100 WALKS IN Greater London

compil

PETER RUDD

The Crowood Press

First published in 1996 by
The Crowood Press Ltd
Ramsbury
Marlborough
Wiltshire SN8 2HR

British Library Cataloguing-in-Publication Data
A catalogue record for this book is
available from the British Library

ISBN 1 85223 951 4

All maps by Janet Powell

Typeset by Carreg Limited, Ross-on-Wye, Herefordshire

Printed by Redwood Books, Trowbridge, Wiltshire

CONTENTS

35.	Ickenham	$4^1/_4$m ($6^3/_4$km)
36.	Limehouse	$4^1/_4$m ($6^3/_4$km)
37.	Alexandra Palace	$4^1/_4$m ($6^3/_4$km)
38.	Tower Precincts	$4^1/_4$m ($6^3/_4$km)
39.	Horton Country Park	$4^1/_4$m ($6^3/_4$km)
40.	Chase Nature Reserve	$4^1/_2$m ($7^1/_4$km)
41.	Bentley Priory Circuit	$4^1/_2$m ($7^1/_4$km)
42.	Bushy Park	$4^1/_2$m ($7^1/_4$km)
43.	Fairlop Waters	$4^1/_2$m ($7^1/_4$km)
44.	Osterley Park	$4^1/_2$m ($7^1/_4$km)
45.	Bedfords Park	$4^1/_2$m ($7^1/_4$km)
46.	Blackheath Common	$4^1/_2$m ($7^1/_4$km)
47.	Trent Park	$4^1/_2$m ($7^1/_4$km)
48.	Syon Park	$4^1/_2$m ($7^1/_4$km)
49.	Selsdon Wood	$4^1/_2$m ($7^1/_4$km)
50.	Hammersmith and Mortlake	$4^3/_4$m ($7^1/_2$km)
51.	… and longer version	$6^3/_4$m (11km)
52.	Hyde Park	$4^3/_4$m ($7^1/_2$km)
53.	Hampstead Heath	$4^3/_4$m ($7^1/_2$km)
54.	Twickenham	$4^3/_4$m ($7^1/_2$km)
55.	Forty Hall	$4^3/_4$m ($7^1/_2$km)
56.	Chelsea and Battersea Park	5m (8km)
57.	Upminster and Cranham	5m (8km)
58.	Hampton Court	5m (8km)
59.	Ealing and Gunnersbury	5m (8km)
60.	Wanstead Park	5m (8km)
61.	Banstead Downs	5m (8km)
62.	Kew Riverside	$5^1/_4$m ($8^1/_2$km)
63.	Addington Hills	$5^1/_4$m ($8^1/_2$km)
64.	Monken Hadley	$5^1/_4$m ($8^1/_2$km)
65.	Roding Valley	$5^1/_4$m ($8^1/_2$km)
66.	Beddington Park	$5^1/_4$m ($8^1/_2$km)
67.	Harefield	$5^1/_4$m ($8^1/_2$km)
68.	Joyden's Wood	$5^1/_2$m ($8^3/_4$km)
69.	Coulsdon Common	$5^1/_2$m ($8^3/_4$km)
70.	Docklands	$5^1/_2$m ($8^3/_4$km)

PUBLISHER'S NOTE

We very much hope that you enjoy the routes presented in this book, which has been compiled with the aim of allowing you to explore the area in the best possible way - on foot.

We strongly recommend that you take the relevant map for the area, and for this reason we list the appropriate Ordnance Survey maps for each route (an A to Z or street map will also be useful for the Central London walks). Whilst the details and descriptions given for each walk were accurate at time of writing, the countryside is constantly changing, and a map will be essential if, for any reason, you are unable to follow the given route. It is good practice to carry a map and use it so that you are always aware of your exact location.

We cannot be held responsible if some of the details in the route descriptions are found to be inaccurate, but should be grateful if walkers would advise us of any major alterations. Please note that whenever you are walking in the countryside you are on somebody else's land, and we must stress that you should *always* keep to established rights of way, and *never* cross fences, hedges or other boundaries unless there is a clear crossing point.

Remember the country code:

Enjoy the country and respect its life and work
Guard against all risk of fire
Fasten all gates
Keep dogs under close control
Keep to public footpaths across all farmland
Use gates and stiles to cross field boundaries
Leave all livestock, machinery and crops alone
Take your litter home
Help to keep all water clean
Protect wildlife, plants and trees
Make no unnecessary noise

The walks are listed by length - from approximately 3 to 12 miles - but the amount of time taken will depend on the fitness of the walkers and the time spent exploring any points of interest along the way. Nearly all the walks are circular and most offer recommendations for refreshments.

Good walking.

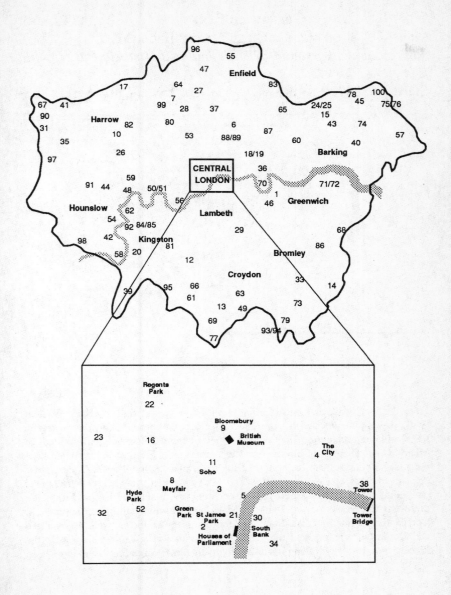

Walk 1   GREENWICH PARK $2^3/_4$m ($4^1/_2$km)

Maps: OS Sheets Landranger 177; Pathfinder 1175.

A circular walk around one of London's Historic Parks, with fine views.

Start: At 383779, Greenwich Pier, next to the Cutty Sark.

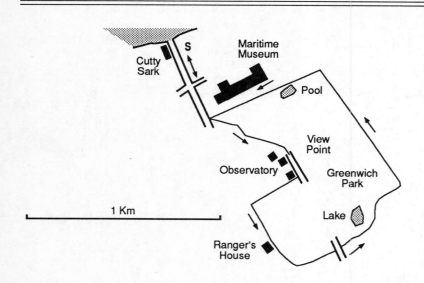

From the Pier, walk alongside the Cutty Sark and then straight up King William Walk, passing the gates of the Royal Naval College on your left. Cross at the traffic lights and continue along King William Walk to enter Greenwich Park through St Mary's Gate. There is an Information Centre near here. From St Mary's Gate, take the first tarmac footpath to the left of the main road. After about 200 yards, at a crossing of paths, take the second right and then turn immediately left on to the fenced path going uphill to the **Old Royal Observatory** and Flamsteed House. From here there are fine views of the National Maritime Museum buildings, Greenwich, Docklands and much of East London. After admiring the views, walk between the Old Royal Observatory and the statue of General Wolfe. Immediately after the Planetarium, turn right along a smaller footpath. Cross a road and continue ahead along this path to Croom Hill Gate. Do not leave the park: instead, turn left and follow the outer boundary path past the rear of McCartney House, General Wolfe's former residence, and the **Ranger's House**.

At the crossing of paths, go forward, continuing to skirt the southern corner of the park. Go past 'The Dell' garden area and a rockery garden, then, at the public conveniences, cross Blackheath Avenue. Here you may wish to make a short detour to the Gate for a view of Blackheath Common, venue for the mass start of the London Marathon. Continue the walk by taking the footpath to the left of the lodge into 'The Flower Gardens'. Keep to the broad path, with the lake and a smaller path to your left. At a junction, with the lake still in view, turn right. Follow the path past a woodland area and the Deer Park to the right, leaving the Flower Gardens through a small iron gate. Go left on the second path, walking parallel to the north-eastern wall of the park. At Maze Hill Gate, with Vanburgh Castle in view, continue ahead, downhill, ignoring a path to the left. At Creed Place Gate, at the northern corner of the park, follow the path to the left around a children's playground and past a boating pool. Continue along the path with the Queen's House and the **National Maritime Museum** buildings to your right. At St Mary's Gate, turn right and retrace the outward route back to the Cutty Sark.

POINTS OF INTEREST:

The Old Royal Observatory – Here it is possible to stand astride the Greenwich Meridian in the courtyard, with one foot in the East and one in the West. There are detailed astronomical displays and you can also watch the famous red Time-Ball drop at the top of Flamsteed House at 1 o'clock.

The Ranger's House – This charming English Heritage red-brick house was built around 1700. It was the residence of seafarer Admiral Hosier and of Philip, the 4th Earl of Chesterfield. From 1814 it provided a home for the Rangers of Greenwich Park. It now houses the Suffolk Collection of Paintings and an Architectural Study Centre.

The National Maritime Museum – The museum houses famous and fascinating displays of Britain's naval history, with model ships, paintings and videos, as well as actual vessels. The gigantic Neptune Hall is particularly impressive. The Palladian-style Queen's House is also well worth a visit.

REFRESHMENTS:

The Gipsy Moth, near the Cutty Sark.
The Bosun's Whistle, restaurant behind the National Maritime Museum Gallery.

Walk 2   St James's Park   2³/₄m (4¹/₂km)

Maps: OS Sheets Landranger 176; Pathfinder 1159 and 1175.
A figure of eight around two Royal Parks.
Start: At 296795, St James's Park Underground Station.

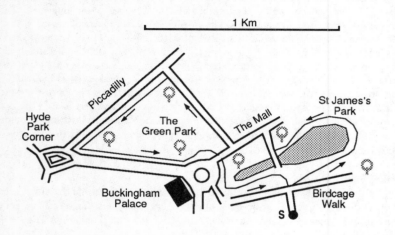

Leaving the station by the Palmer Street exit, turn right and then right again into Petty France. Cross Petty France at the pedestrian crossing and walk down Queen Anne's Gate, heading for St James's Park.

Cross Birdcage Walk by means of the pedestrian crossing and walk into **St James's Park,** turning immediately right after passing the two information boards. Follow the path to the edge of the lake (Duck Island and the Birdkeeper's Cottage can be seen ahead) and then continue around its eastern end, with Horse Guards Parade to the right.

Fork left where there is a Silver Jubilee Walkway indicator so as to stay close to the lake, then walk to the left of 'The Cake House', where refreshments may be obtained. Now keep close to the lake until you are parallel with the bridge, then turn right and leave St James's Park through the iron gates on to The Mall.

Cross by the lights and turn left to walk along The Mall (which has seen numerous royal processions and, since 1994, the finish of the London Marathon). Buckingham Palace can be seen ahead and Clarence House and Lancaster House are to the right.

Shortly before reaching the Queen Victoria Memorial (in front of Buckingham Palace) turn right down Queen's Walk, a drive running between the eastern edge of **The Green Park** and the grounds of Lancaster House. Continue along Queen's Walk until you are close to Piccadilly and the Ritz Hotel. Do not go through the gate: instead, turn left to follow the path running parallel with Piccadilly, going along the north-western perimeter of Green Park.

Keep on this path for about $^1/_3$ mile, then leave Green Park temporarily through the Wellington Place Gate. Use the subway to reach Wellington Place and Hyde Park Corner. This must be one of London's most famous traffic islands and is worth exploring in detail. There are two war memorials, as well as the Wellington Statue and the Wellington Arch.

Return to Green Park using the same subway steps (exit 12). Continue forward along the southern perimeter of Green Park, with Constitution Hill and the wall of Buckingham Palace Gardens to your right.

As you pass Buckingham Palace, go through Canada Gate and then left along The Mall for a short distance. Cross The Mall and enter St James's Park once more, walking towards the lake. Turn right and walk round the western end of the lake. Keep to the path closest to the lake until you reach the central bridge once again. Here, turn right and leave the park by the St Anne's Gate exit, reversing the outward route to return to St James's Park Station.

POINTS OF INTEREST:

St James's Park – The name of the park originates from a 13th-century leper colony on the site dedicated to St James. The park has numerous royal connections, but in Queen Anne's reign was the haunt of prostitutes! Today it is home to a variety of waterfowl, including the famous pelicans.

The Green Park – Though neither as scenic nor as popular as St James's Park, Green Park has a sedate character all of its own and provides a peaceful retreat from the surrounding traffic. It forms part of a 'green chain' across central London, linking St James's Park with Hyde Park.

REFRESHMENTS:

The Cake House, St James's Park.

Walk 3   THEATRELAND $2^{3}/_{4}$m ($4^{1}/_{2}$ km)

Maps: OS Sheets Landranger 176; Pathfinder 1159.

A walk through the Central London shops and entertainment districts.

Start: At 295806, Piccadilly Circus Underground Station.

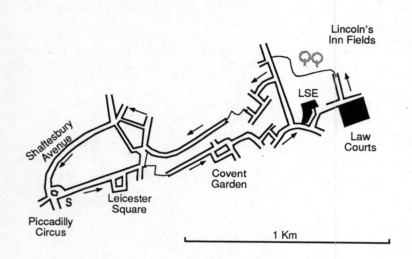

Leave the Underground Station by Subway 3 (Eros/Lower Regent Street). Walk between the Eros Statue and the Criterion Theatre along Coventry Street, then continue along the northern edge of Leicester Square. Maintain direction down Cranbourn Street, passing the Hippodrome. Cross Charing Cross Road and go down the alleyway (St Martin's Court) between Leicester Square Station and Wyndham's Theatre. Follow this right and left to emerge into St Martin's Lane at the Albery Theatre. Cross St Martin's Lane and continue up New Row. Cross Bedford Street and continue to reach the Covent Garden Market area. Walk through the Market, with its numerous small shops, market stalls and street entertainers, to reach the **London Transport Museum** (in the far right-hand corner). From the Museum exit, turn right and then right again to leave the Market area along Russell Street. Walk past the **Theatre Museum**, cross

Bow Street and then turn right down Catherine Street, passing the front entrance of the Theatre Royal. At the crossroads, turn left down Tavistock Street, then go right, down part of Drury Lane, to reach the Aldwych Theatre. From here cross the road to go left down Aldwych. The route now leaves the entertainment district temporarily: cross Kingsway at the lights and, shortly, turn left down Houghton Street, passing between buildings of the London School of Economics. At the corner, go right down Clement's Inn Passage and left along Grange Court. On reaching Carey Street, turn right to pass the rear of the Royal Courts of Justice.

Go left down Serle Street, then continue to Lincoln's Inn Fields. Go through the gate and bear left, walking around the Fields until you reach the exit with a fountain at the far corner. Go diagonally over the crossroads and under the arches, going down Remnant Street. Cross at the lights and walk left down Kingsway for about 100 yards to reach Wild Court. Turn right here, and at the end turn left. Opposite Kemble House, turn right and go down Kemble Street. At the crossroads, go right to walk along another section of Drury Lane. Use the pedestrian crossing and continue to Martlett Court, where a sign warns that 'hawkers, traders & others are prohibited from calling shouting or using any bell or other instruments on this estate'. Walk along Martlett Court and then go right down Crown Court. Turn left at Broad Court to reach Bow Street, passing the statue of the 'Young Dancer' by Plazzota. Go over Bow Street and walk down Floral Street, with the Royal Opera House to your left. Cross James Street and continue along the cobbled part of Floral Street to reach Garrick Street. Turn right, cross at the lights and bear right along Upper St Martin's Lane. Turn left at West Street and follow this around, passing St Martin's Theatre. At the end, turn left to cross Cambrdge Circus to reach Shaftesbury Avenue (to the left of the Palace Theatre). Walk along the Avenue, passing more theatres, cinemas and restaurants to reach Piccadilly Circus once more.

POINTS OF INTEREST:

London Transport Museum – The museum provides fascinating displays on London's transport history. There is also a 'Transport Cafe' and a shop with books, videos, posters and postcards.

The Theatre Museum – The National Museum for the Performing Arts, this building was opened as a museum in 1987. It is part of the Victoria and Albert Museum.

REFRESHMENTS:

The walker is spoilt for choice on this route. The Leicester Square and Covent Garden areas are probably the best in London for wining and dining.

Walk 4   **THE CITY OF LONDON**   3m (4³/₄km)

Maps: OS Sheets Landranger 177; Pathfinder 1159.

City institutions old and new.

Start: At 333816, Liverpool Street Station.

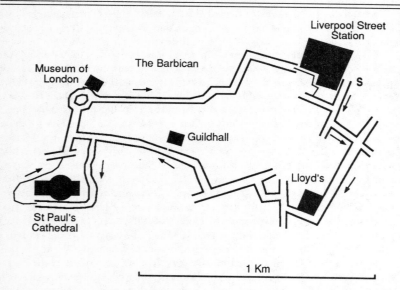

Leave Liverpool Street Station by the Bishopsgate exit (next to platform 18). Turn right to walk down Bishopsgate, then turn left down Houndsditch. Shortly, turn right down St Mary Axe and follow this past the newly-rebuilt Baltic Exchange. Pass the Church of St Andrew Undershaft, with the ultra-modern Lloyds building, designed by Richard Rogers and completed in 1986, ahead. Cross Leadenhall Street and walk down Lime Street, to the left of the Lloyds building. At the corner of the building go right down Leadenhall Place and walk through the covered Leadenhall Market.

Turn right onto Gracechurch Street and, at the lights, go left down Cornhill. Pass another City church, St Michael Cornhill, on the left, then turn right down Finch Lane. This brings you to Threadneedle Street where you should turn left to view the Stock Exchange, the Bank of England and the Royal Exchange. By the Wellington Statue there is a Silver Jubilee Walkway information post.

With the Mansion House in front of you, at the corner of the Bank of England, turn right down Princes Street. On the left a plaque commemorates the fact that the first postmark in the world was struck near here in 1661. At the lights, turn left to go down Gresham Street. The Guildhall and the **Guild Church of St Lawrence Jewry** can be seen on the right. Continue down Gresham Street until you reach Foster Lane. Turn left here and walk past the entrance to Goldsmiths' Hall. At the end of Foster Lane, cross Cheapside and walk to the left of the Churchyard of St Paul's Cathedral along a road called 'New Change'. At the crossroads, turn right into Cannon Street and St Paul's Churchyard. Walk around the west front and the north side of the Cathedral, so almost completing a circuit of the building.

After passing the Chapter House, go up Cathedral Steps to the St Paul's Shopping Centre. Turn right to reach an entrance to St Paul's Underground Station. Cross Newgate Street and walk down the left side of St Martin's Le-Grande. Turn left at the roundabout, then go immediately left up the steps to reach the **Museum of London**. Walk to the right, around Nettleton Court, to reach the Museum entrance and shop.

If you are not going into the Museum, turn right along the Bastion High Walk. Keep forward on this walkway, with the Barbican development to the left. As you pass The Podium Inn, the walkway becomes the St Alphage High Walk: follow this to pass to the left of The Plough then go left along the Moorfields High Walk. Go down the escalator to Moorgate Station, continue ahead through Moor Place, and then turn left onto Moorfields. Cross at the traffic lights in order to go right down South Place: walk along here to reach the Broadgate entrance to Liverpool Street Station.

POINTS OF INTEREST:
Guild Church of St Lawrence Jewry – This is the guild church of the Corporation of the City of London: the Lord Mayor worships here. The medieval church on the site was destroyed in the Great Fire of 1666 and Wren was responsible for the design of the new building. This in turn suffered bomb damage in 1940, but has been restored in Wren's style. The 'Jewry' in the name is a reference to the fact that up until the late 13th century this neighbourhood was the Jewish Quarter of London.
The Museum of London – Opened in 1976 as part of the Barbican complex, this Museum houses detailed displays on the history of London from prehistoric times to the present day. The exhibits include the Lord Mayor's Coach.

REFRESHMENTS:
There are several options along the route, perhaps the best of which is the London Museum Cafeteria.

Walk 5   VICTORIA EMBANKMENT   3m (4³/₄km)

Maps: OS Sheets Landranger 176 or 177; Pathfinder 1159 and 1175.

A walk along the Thames Embankment.

Start: At 303797, Westminster Underground Station.

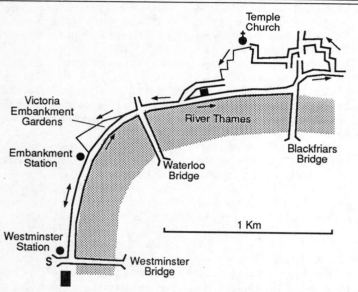

This easy walk takes you along the famous Victoria Embankment by the Thames. This section of the Embankment always provides an interesting stroll: as well as views across to the South Bank and activity on the river itself, there are numerous statues, memorials and plaques to be seen. The walk turns back at Blackfriars to visit the Temple area with its notable legal institutions.

Leave Westminster Station by the Embankment exit. Cross the road at the lights close to Westminster Bridge and turn left. Now follow the Thames-side footpath on Victoria Embankment for about 1¹/₂ miles: the route passes under Hungerford railway bridge, then reaches **Cleopatra's Needle**. From here it proceeds under Waterloo Bridge and passes two dragons marking the boundary of the City of London.

Keep ahead until you reach the northern end of Blackfriars Bridge. There, go down the steps (signposted as the 'Thames Path', subway exit 5). Where there is a crossing of subways, turn right and immediately left to leave by exit 2. Go left and follow the pavement around an entrance to Blackfriars Station. From the lights at the junction with Puddle Dock (very close to the Mermaid Theatre), cross and head up St Andrews Hill. After passing the Cockpit Inn, turn left into Ireland Yard. At the end of this passageway, turn right along another called Church Entry (the site of the Former Great Dominican Priory of Blackfriars) and then left along Carter Lane and right at Ludgate Broadway. Upon reaching Pilgrim Street, turn left and walk between the bollards. Go down the steps at the rear of the City Thameslink Station and turn left at the main road. Cross at the lights and go down Bridewell Place. Follow this around to the left, and at the end turn right into Tudor Street.

At Temple Lane, continue through the doorway next to the arch into Inner Temple. From the car park in Kings Bench Row, turn right and, shortly, left down a passageway (just before the Francis Taylor Building). Now walk through Church Court to pass the **Temple Church**.

At the end of the court, go through the first set of arches and continue through one more arched passage (Pump Court) to reach Middle Temple Lane. Go left for about 20 yards, and then right along the pavement into Fountain Court. Leave this rather picturesque court by the steps on the left, and turn half-right at the next set of steps to reach a gate at Temple Place. Cross the road and go through another gate to walk through the Temple Section of Victoria Embankment Gardens.

At the end of these gardens, bear right and then left along Temple Place. This leads on to the northern side of Victoria Embankment: pass under Waterloo Bridge and, after crossing Savoy Place, bear right along the tarmac path into Victoria Embankment Gardens. The gardens provide a pleasant finale to the walk: Embankment Station is just beyond their western end. From the Station, Circle and District Line trains return you to Westminster.

POINTS OF INTEREST:

Cleopatra's Needle – This 60 foot obelisk was presented by Mahommed Ali, Viceroy of Egypt, to Britain in 1819. It was erected in 1878.

Temple Church – Church Court provides a tranquil paved area between Middle and Inner Temple. The Church itself dates from 1185, with some 13th-century additions.

REFRESHMENTS:

St Brides Tavern, Bridewell Place.
The Tea House, Victoria Embankment Gardens.

Walk 6   **STOKE NEWINGTON**   3m (4¾km)

Maps: OS Sheets Landranger 176 or 177; Pathfinder 1159.
A walk through North London parks, streets, and a cemetery.
Start: At 314868, Finsbury Park Station.

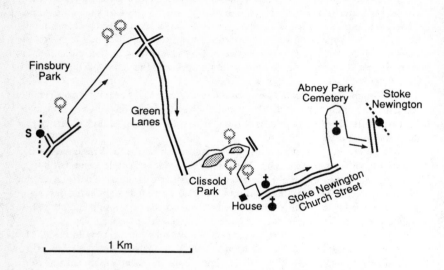

Cross the right-hand side of Station Place to reach the main Seven Sisters Road. Turn left and walk along the road until an entrance to Finsbury Park appears on the left. Now walk along the main park road which curves right to run parallel with the Seven Sisters Road. Where the park road curves left, bear right along the path through the Manor House Gates to reach a road junction. Go right, across Seven Sisters Road, and walk along Green Lanes.

After about ½ mile, shortly after passing the Reservoir Works and crossing Lordship Park, go left through a gate into **Clissold Park**. Take the first path on the left and follow it to the left of the lakes. At the end of the first lake bear right on a broad, tree-lined path signposted to the Information Centre. Stay on this until you reach the rear of Clissold House and then turn left. Pass to the left of Old St Mary's

Church and then go right to a gate. Use the footpath behind the church to reach Stoke Newington Church Street. Turn left and walk along the Street for approximately $^1/_3$ mile, through the older part of Stoke Newington, until an entrance to **Abney Park Cemetery** appears on the left.

Enter the Cemetery, and from the Booth memorials keep left along the main track, following it around the cemetery to where it curves back round near the northern end of the grounds. There are several minor paths leading to the chapel in the centre of the grounds. After almost a full circuit of the cemetery, when you are level with the eastern side of the chapel, turn left along a gravel track to reach the Stoke Newington High Street exit. Turn left and walk up the High Street and Stamford Hill to reach Stoke Newington railway station from where trains will return you directly to Finsbury Park Station.

POINTS OF INTEREST:

Clissold Park – The Park and House were opened to the public in 1899. The lakes are populated by several bird species. The two churches near the Park are both confusingly called St Mary's. Old St Mary's dates from the 16th century, while the more recent St Mary's, designed by Gilbert Scott, was built in 1858.

Abney Park Cemetery – The Abney Park Cemetery Trust, together with Hackney Council, are working to restore the cemetery. It dates from 1840 and is now something of a haven for wildlife. Famous individuals buried here include William and Catherine Booth, founders of the Salvation Army. The Chapel and a memorial to Isaac Watts, the hymn-writer, are situated in the centre of the grounds.

REFRESHMENTS:

There are many options in Finsbury Park and Stoke Newington.

Walk 7   **DOLLIS VALLEY**   3m (4³/₄km)

Maps: OS Sheets Landranger 176; Pathfinder 1140.
An easy brookside trail between Woodside Park and Barnet.
Start: At 257926, Woodside Park Underground Station.

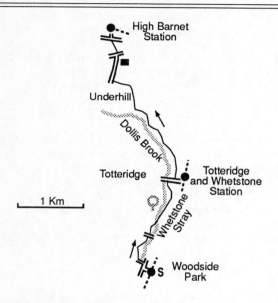

Leave Woodside Park Station from the northbound (trains to High Barnet) platform.
Walk down the approach road, turn right along Holden Road and then left along
Tillingham Way. After nearly 200 yards, turn right on to the Dollis Valley Green
Walk. The Walk is indicated by a signpost next to a white gate and follows the course
of the **Dollis Brook**. Follow the Walk past a sports ground and over a road called
Laurel View to reach Whetstone Stray. Stay on the tarmac path (which also serves as
a cycleway) across the Stray. At Totteridge Lane, cross to the parade of shops and
turn right. (The village of **Totteridge** is to the west of this point). Shortly, before
Totteridge and Whetstone Underground Station, turn left at another Dollis Valley
Green Walk sign. Cross Brook Farm Open Space where there is the luxury of both a
footpath and a cycleway: where these eventually diverge, keep left on the cycleway,
staying close to the brook.

Turn right after entering Barnet playing fields and keep to the right-hand side of the park. After about 400 yards the path meets a broader tarmac track and Underhill, the home of Barnet Football Club, can be seen ahead. Turn left along the track and walk between the playing fields to reach Barnet Lane. Turn right and, at the T-junction at the end of Barnet Lane, cross and continue forward along a footpath. Use the pedestrian crossing on Barnet Hill to reach the entrance road to High Barnet Underground Station from where Northern Line trains will return you to the start.

POINTS OF INTEREST:

Dollis Brook – The brook flows south from Arkley through various parks and open spaces in the Borough of Barnet to join Mutton Brook and the River Brent.

Totteridge – The main part of the village is about a mile west of the Dollis Brook. Totteridge Lane has a number of fine houses and is a conservation area. St Andrew's Church dates from the 18th century.

REFRESHMENTS:

None directly on the route, but there are shops at Totteridge, and Barnet High Street is beyond the station at the end of the walk.

Walk 8 **MAYFAIR SQUARES** 3m (4³/₄km)

Maps: OS Sheets Landranger 176; Pathfinder 1159.
W1 Streets and squares.
Start: At 275820, Marylebone Station.

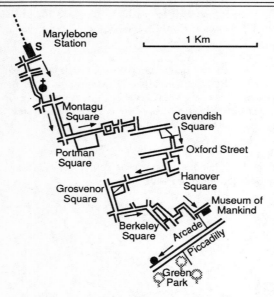

This stroll includes some of the most famous squares of London W1. The squares often provide quiet retreats from the busy streets and there are many interesting and historical buildings, along with numerous blue plaques.

Leave Marylebone Station (main line or underground), turning right into Melcombe Place and then left down Harewood Avenue. Cross the busy Marylebone Road at the lights and continue forward along Enford Street. Walk around St Mary's Church and continue down Wyndham Place, passing the Duke of Wellington Inn on the left.

At the T-junction you are at the northern end of Bryanston Square: turn left and, after about 200 yards, right to enter Montagu Square. Cross George Street and continue along Montagu Street. At the end turn left into Upper Berkeley Street.

Cross Gloucester Place and continue along the northern edge of Portman Square. Go over Baker Street to reach Fitzhardinge Street and walk around the northern (left) side of Manchester Square. Hertford House, the home of the Wallace Collection is located here.

Leave the square via Hinde Street and continue along Bentinck Street. At the end, go right down Welbeck Street and at the lights turn left into Wigmore Street. At the second set of traffic lights, cross over and walk around a section of Cavendish Square Gardens, leaving by Holles Street, to the left of Lewis's Store.

Cross Oxford Street and continue down Harewood Place to reach Hanover Square. At the far right-hand corner of the square, turn right along Brook Street, admiring the fine examples of 18th-century architecture. Follow the Street for nearly $1/3$ mile, to reach **Grosvenor Square**. Go diagonally across Grosvenor Square Gardens and then head left down South Audley Street. Now take the second left, Mount Street.

At the end of Mount Street, turn right to reach Berkeley Square. Walk around Berkeley Square Gardens and leave (at the far left corner) along Berkeley Street. Almost immediately, turn left up Hay Hill, then left along Dover Street and right along Grafton Street. On reaching New Bond Street, go right and then left down Burlington Gardens to reach the **Museum of Mankind**.

From the Museum retrace your steps for a short distance, then go down the splendid Burlington Arcade (if the Arcade is closed use Old Bond Street). At the end, turn right and complete the route by walking along Piccadilly for a short distance to reach Green Park Underground Station from where underground trains run back to Marylebone.

POINTS OF INTEREST:

Grosvenor Square – Compared to the other squares, this seems to have an air of openness about it. Indeed it is the largest square in London apart from Lincoln's Inn Fields. The Square has many American connections: there is a statue of Franklin D Roosevelt and the American Embassy is on the western side.

Museum of Mankind – This building, No. 6, Burlington Gardens, was constructed between 1866 and 1869. Since 1970 it has housed the British Museum's Department of Ethnography. There are displays relating to non-Western societies and cultures.

REFRESHMENTS:

The Thornbury Castle, Enford Street.
Duke of Wellington, Crawford Street.
Cafe de Colombia, Museum of Mankind.

Walk 9   **BLOOMSBURY**   3m (4$\frac{3}{4}$km)

Maps: OS Sheets Landranger 176; Pathfinder 1159.
A circular walk of streets and squares of WC1.
Start: At 296826, Euston Station Forecourt.

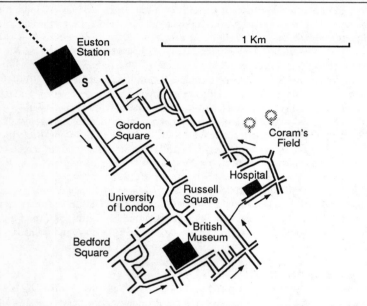

From the front of Euston Station, cross Euston Road and proceed rightwards to reach Gordon Street. Turn left here and continue forwards as Gordon Street enters Bloomsbury and becomes **Gordon Square**. At the end of the square, turn left and then (near the corner of Tavistock Square) turn right along Bedford Way.

At the end of Bedford Way, cross over and bear right to walk round the western side of **Russell Square**, leaving at Montagu Place, on the right. Cross Malet Street and, at the end of Montagu Place, cross Gower Street and walk forwards and leftwards around Bedford Square. Leave this attractive Georgian square (which is actually oval-shaped) by walking through Adeline Place.

Cross Bedford Avenue and, at the next junction, turn left along Great Russell Street, passing Congress House, the headquarters of the Trades Union Congress. Cross

24

Bloomsbury Street and pass the British Museum and Library, to the left. Shortly, turn right down Bury Place, passing Pied Bull Yard.

At the end, turn left and walk along Bloomsbury Way. Walk past Bloomsbury Square and turn left at the lights to go along Southampton Row. When you reach the Bedford Hotel, cross and walk down an alleyway (Cosmo Place). Cross Queen Square and contine down Great Ormond Street, passing the famous Hospital for Sick Children.

Turn left into Lamb's Conduit Street and, at Guilford Place, keep left into Guilford Street. Cross over and go right down Lansdowne Terrace. Follow the Terrace leftwards, and then bear right down Hunter Street. At the end of the modern Brunswick Development, turn left into Handel Street. This bears right and becomes Kenton Street: at the end, turn left and almost immediately right down Marchmont Street. Shortly, bear left into Cartwright Gardens, an elegant crescent with hotels.

At Burton Place, turn left and then go right along Burton Street. At the junction with Flaxman Terrace, turn left to pass through Woburn Walk, with its old-fashioned, bow-fronted shops. There is a plaque indicating that W B Yeats lodged in one of these buildings from 1865 to 1919. Go right along Upper Woburn Place and left at Euston Road to return to Euston Station.

POINTS OF INTEREST:
Gordon Square – The Square has strong associations with the 'Bloomsbury Group' of intellectuals. Former residents include Virginia Woolf, Bertrand Russell and John Maynard Keynes.

Russell Square – The largest of the Bloomsbury squares, this area is now partially surrounded by University of London buildings, with the tower of Senate House nearby.

REFRESHMENTS:
There are numerous inns and restaurants on the route, particularly in Southampton Row and in the vicinity of Lamb's Conduit Street.

Walk 10   HARROW-ON-THE-HILL   3¼m (5¼km)

Maps: OS Sheets Landranger 176; Pathfinder 1158.

A short, hilly village walk on pavements, footpaths and fields.

Start: At 153880, Harrow-on-the-Hill Station (Rail and Underground).

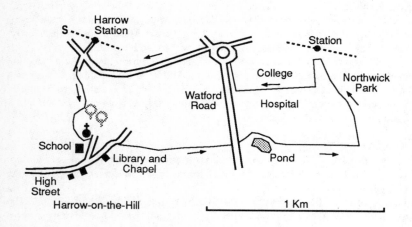

Leave **Harrow-on-the-Hill** Station by the Lowlands Road and Roxeth exit. Cross the main road and go up Lansdowne Road and the footpath on the edge of the green to the wooded area at the top of the hill. Turn right along the fenced footpath and then left along a broad path by the churchyard. At the end of this path, on a clear day, you can admire the view towards Windsor. Also note the stone commemorating 'Lines written by Byron at this place'.

Walk past St Mary's Church, which was consecrated in 1094, and leave by the lych gate. Turn right and walk down Church Hill. The original building of **Harrow School**, dating from 1615, is on your right. The school has, of course, expanded considerably since then. From the bottom of Church Hill you may wish to briefly detour right to explore Harrow High Street.

To continue the walk, turn sharp left from Church Hill and cross the road to walk past the Vaughan Library, designed by Sir George Gilbert Scott and named after a former Headmaster, and the School Chapel, also designed by Scott. Follow the hill to the right and then turn right where a sign indicates a footpath to Watford Road. This lane, called Football Lane, takes you past more school buildings and on to the playing fields. At this point, go half-left across the sports fields, leaving over a stile in the far left-hand corner. Admire the view of the school and Harrow-on-the-Hill behind you, and then cross Watford Road to join 'The Ducker Footpath'. Follow this around to the municipal pitch and putt course, and then keep to the left, by the trees and a fence. When you reach the end (or the entrance) of the pitch and putt course, turn left along a concrete path by a small stream, next to Northwick Park playing fields.

This path leaves the field at Northwick Park Station where those wishing to end the walk can catch an Underground train. To continue back to Harrow on foot, turn sharp left and walk along the fenced path, passing two tall chimneys. Follow the path to the right to walk between Northwick Park Hospital and the Harrow Campus of the University of Westminster. Turn right at the dual carriageway, then use the subway at the roundabout. Go up the steps on to Kenton Road. After about $1/2$ mile and one set of traffic lights, this road brings you to a Memorial Cross, the green and Harrow-on-the-Hill Station.

POINTS OF INTEREST:

Harrow-on-the-Hill – The existence of the surrounding fields helps Harrow maintain its semi-rural village character. The village is over 200 feet above sea level and there are some splendid views. There are several interesting buildings in the High Street, but the 'village' is dominated by its famous public school.

Harrow School – The earliest building has been dated to 1615, but there may well have been a school in the village before then. There have been many famous pupils at the school, including Lord Byron and Sir Winston Churchill. The pupils still wear the famous flat straw hat which they take off and carry when walking on the public roads.

REFRESHMENTS:

The Kings Head, Harrow-on-the-Hill can be found on the High Street, just off the route.

There are also numerous possibilities near Harrow Station.

Walk 11   SOHO AND CHINATOWN   3¼m (5¼km)

Maps: OS Sheets Landranger 176; Pathfinder 1159.

A walk along busy, cosmopolitan streets.

Start: At 295818, Goodge Street Underground Station.

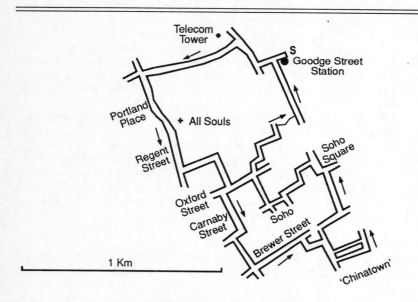

The early part of this walk is north of Oxford Street, with the later stages going through the heart of Soho via Carnaby Street and Gerrard Street, returning to Goodge Street through a number of alleyways.

From the station, turn left and immediately left again at Tottenham Street. Cross Whitfield Street and at Charlotte Street turn right: the Telecom Tower looms up to the left. Cross at the lights and go left down Howland Street. Continue ahead at the next set of lights into New Cavendish Street, passing the University of Westminster Science and Engineering Buildings. Go across Great Portland Street and Hallam Street to reach the traffic lights at Portland Place. Turn left and walk past the BBC building and All Souls Church, Langham Place. Continue along Regent Street to reach Great Castle Street (the fifth street on the left). Cross Great Portland Street and go along

Market Place. Turn right along Great Titchfield Street, cross Oxford Street and go down the steps directly opposite (Ramillies Street). At the end (Great Marlborough Street) turn right and walk to a large black and white timber-framed building. There, go left to enter Soho and pedestriansed **Carnaby Street**. At its end, go right, very briefly, then left down Upper John Street. Continue as this becomes the western side of Golden Square and Lower John Street. Turn left along Brewer Street (where there are some remnants of Soho's sex industry), then take the third street, Rupert Street, on the right. At the Gielgud Theatre (formerly The Globe) cross Shaftesbury Avenue and go briefly left, and then right, down Wardour Steet. Almost immediately go left into Gerrard Street. At the end, go right down Newport Place and right again along Lisle Street. At its end, turn right into Wardour Street to complete this small circuit of London's Chinatown.

Cross Oxford Street and go down Wardour Street, passing St Anne's Church. At the corner, turn right along Old Compton Street, often regarded as the heart of Soho. At the second crossroads, turn left into Frith Street, passing Ronnie Scott's Jazz Club and a former residence of Mozart, to reach Soho Square. Exit left along Carlisle Street and go left again into Dean Street. Almost immediately, turn right down a passageway called St Anne's Court. At the end, continue along Broadwick Street, then turn right along **Poland Street** to reach Oxford Street. Go right, but soon turn left down Wells Street. At the crossroads, turn right down Eastcastle Street and at its end turn left into Newman Street. Soon, turn right down Newman Passage but where the road goes right, continue down the paved alleyway. Go straight across Rathbone Street and down Percy Passage. Cross, going slightly left and forwards down Windmill Street. Follow this around to the left as it becomes Whitfield Street, passing Pollock's Toy Museum. Turn right at Tottenham Street: Goodge Street Station is just to the right.

POINTS OF INTEREST:

Carnaby Street – One of London's most famous shopping streets, this now seems to be more of a tourist attraction than a serious fashion centre. The alleyways and side streets provide interesting diversions.

Poland Street – This was one of London's most fashionable streets in the 18th century and some houses of that period remain. Named after the King of Poland Tavern which used to exist here, the street has had a number of famous residents including Shelley and William Blake.

REFRESHMENTS:

There are many options on this route, most notably the diverse culinary delights of Gerrard Street and Lisle Street.

Walk 12   THE WANDLE TRAIL   3¼m (5¼km)

Maps: OS Sheets Landranger 176; Pathfinder 1191.
A riverside walk through three South London parks.
Start: At 283676, Mitcham Junction Railway Station.

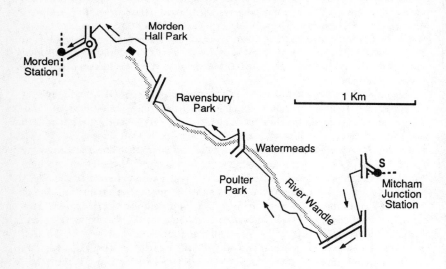

This route mainly follows the course of the River Wandle from Mitcham to Morden, going through Poulter, Ravensbury and Morden Hall Parks. It starts from Mitcham Junction Station (trains run here from Victoria) and finishes at Morden Underground Station on the Northern line.

From Mitcham Junction Station, turn left and walk along the station drive to the main road. Cross the road with care, and turn left to go over the railway bridge. At the end of the bridge, turn right along a path called Aspen Gardens. Keep on this as it is signposted leftwards as a public footpath. Walk along a row of houses and over two side roads. At the next road, near a bus stop, bear right and then right again at the Goat Inn to walk along Goat Road.

Cross Wates Way and, soon, reach a bridge over the **River Wandle**. Turn right down Watermead Lane. The lane passes a row of houses and then becomes a footpath, joined at a metal kissing gate. Follow this riverside path, passing Poulter Park on the left. After about $1/3$ mile, the river bends sharply right and the path turns to gravel and leaves the riverside temporarily, following the edge of a wood which is part of a National Trust Nature Reserve (with restricted access) called 'Watermeads'.

At the Bishopsford Road, turn right, following the sign for Ravensbury and Morden Hall Park. Cross the bridge over the river and, at Riverside Drive, cross and go down the footpath at the end of the red-brick wall. This path follows the northern bank of the river through **Ravensbury Park**. After crossing the second footbridge, turn left along a gravel path so as to keep close to the river. Walk past several flower and rose beds, and another footbridge still keeping close to the river. The path then takes you over a footbridge and leftwards to reach a road. Turn right, crossing the road just before the Surrey Arms to enter **Morden Hall Park** through a wooden gate. Keep forward along the main path which swings left and then crosses a white ornamental bridge. The rear of Morden Hall, which is not open to the public, can be seen ahead. Turn left immediately after the bridge to detour to a number of outbuildings including the Snuff Mill Environmental Centre, a cafe and a garden centre.

To continue the walk bear right along a gravel path after crossing the white bridge. This path takes you over two footbridges and then forks. Take the left branch and, after crossing the next bridge, keep left to reach a gate at the main road. Turn left, cross at the lights and then bear right down the A24 at the roundabout to reach Morden Underground Station.

POINTS OF INTEREST:
River Wandle – The river once provided water and power for a local textile industry. Much of the area close to the river is now being developed for recreational use. The 'Wandle Trail' extends from Carshalton to Lambeth.
Ravensbury Park – Ravensbury was one of four medieval manors in Mitcham. Not much remains of the original Manor House, but much of the Mill (near Morden Road) does still exist.
Morden Hall Park – The Estate was left to the National Trust in 1941. The Park provides meadowland, marsh and woodland habitats. The buildings near the Hall include craft workshops, a garden centre, an environmental centre and a cafe.

REFRESHMENTS:
The Riverside Cafe, Morden Hall.

Walk 13   **RIDDLESDOWN** $3\frac{1}{4}$m ($5\frac{1}{4}$km)
Maps: OS Sheets Landranger 187; Pathfinder 1191 and 1207.
Easy downland walking.
Start: At 325605, the car park, Riddlesdown Road, off Mitchley
Avenue, Purley.

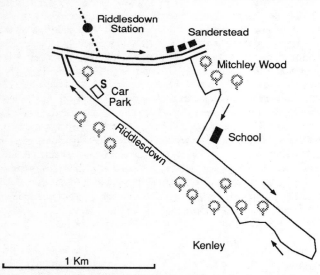

An alternative start to this walk is Riddlesdown Railway Station, which has a limited
weekday service from London Victoria.

From the car park, walk back along the entrance road and leave the Common by
continuing down Riddlesdown Road. At the crossroads, cross and turn right to walk
along Mitchley Avenue. (If you are starting from Riddlesdown Station leave the East
Grinstead-bound platform and turn immediately right along a tarmac footpath at the
exit. Ignore another path to the left and continue up this footpath to emerge at Mitchley
Avenue).

Follow Mitchley Avenue for about $\frac{1}{3}$ mile, then, approximately 200 yards after
a small parade of shops, go right up a footpath, just before a doctor's surgery. This is
not signposted but it is a public footpath.

The path heads uphill along the edge of Mitchley Wood: behind there is a good view of Sanderstead. At the top of the hill the path curves right along the top edge of the field. After about 100 yards, go left through a gap in the trees and immediately right along a gravel track, passing Riddlesdown High School. After passing the school entrance, turn left along a bridleway towards Hamsey Green. Follow the bridleway for just over $^1/_3$ mile, passing a triangulation point. You may see gliders over this part of the downs: they take off and land at nearby Kenley Aerodrome.

Shortly after the bridleway leaves the row of trees and begins to curve left to Hamsey Green, bear right along a less well-defined grass path. Go over a crossing path and keep ahead to meet a junction of six footpaths, between the trees. At the junction, take the first path on the right to begin the return across **Riddlesdown**, walking in a north-easterly direction with a fence to your left and an open field to your right. Where the fence ends, continue forwards and slightly downhill, passing a bench constructed from a tree trunk split in half. After 100 yards the path forks: keep left, going along the steeper downhill path and taking in the views over Riddlesdown and Kenley. When the path reaches a fence, go under or around the small wooden barrier and then turn right along the edge of a clearing. Follow the grass path for nearly a mile as it crosses other paths and passes between a number of fence sections. This track is one of the main routes along Riddlesdown. It eventually converges with a more well-defined stone track: follow this over the crest of the down, continuing along it to reach Riddlesdown Road at the car park.

POINTS OF INTEREST:

Riddlesdown – The chalk downland is one of several commons in the area, collectively known as 'Coulsdon Commons'. Maintained by the Corporation of London, Riddlesdown is both an ancient monument and a Site of Special Scientific Interest. The walk route runs along the crest of the downland, though it is worth detouring occasionally to explore the woodlands on the southern slopes.

REFRESHMENTS:

None on the route, so you will need to take your own.

Walk 14   CHELSFIELD AND MAYPOLE   3¼m (5¼km)

Maps: OS Sheets Landranger 177; Pathfinder 1192.

An easy village ramble.

Start: At 483642, the Five Bells Inn, Church Road, Chelsfield.

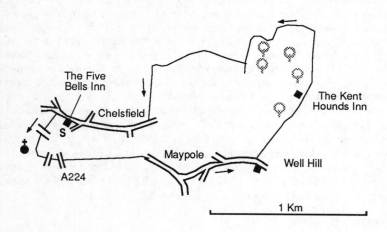

From the Five Bells Inn, walk along Warren Road, passing the Primary School and the Wesleyan Chapel. Cross and go left down the public footpath opposite Chelsfield Lane. Cross the A224, with care, and keep ahead to reach **Chelsfield Church**. Walk along the left side of the churchyard, and then go left, at the corner, along another public footpath, going through the church car park. Cross a minor road, rejoin the footpath (just to the right) and cross the A224, with care, again. The path now crosses a field, following the line of telegraph poles. At the hedge, ignore the arrow pointing left, keeping ahead across the next two fields, still following the telegraph poles. At the next corner, go through the hedge and cross a stile. Cross three more stiles, visible ahead, to reach a lane near Maple House.

Turn right along the lane towards Maypole village and, after about 150 yards, turn left into Jubilee Road. At the end, next to Forkways Cottage, turn right along the road for about 100 yards, then fork left up a public footpath opposite the Rock and

Fountain car park. Walk past a number of attractive cottages and then bear right along a public bridleway where the lane begins to descend. Ignore a track going left, staying on the bridleway to reach the Kent Hounds Inn.

Now follow a narrow, tree-lined footpath to the right of the inn. Cross a lane and a stile near a row of cottages and follow the path beyond downhill along the edge of a wood. Cross the field corner and walk along the left edge of the field for about 80 yards before following the path to the left into the trees. Follow the yellow waymarkers, passing under the electricity lines, to reach a junction of paths next to a stable block. Turn left and follow the yellow waymarkers along a field edge, through a small orchard and across another field. Go through a hedge, down six steps and walk left, and then right, along the field edges.

Follow the path to the left through a corner of the wood and then walk forward, with a large open field to your right and the wood to your immediate left. At the next marker post, at a corner of the wood, turn right to walk along another field edge. About 30 yards into the next field, bear half-left at the waymarker to head diagonally across the field. Continue along the path between the hedgerows to reach a road. Turn right and walk along Bucks Cross Road back into Chelsfield, passing Chelsfield Park Hospital on the way.

POINTS OF INTEREST:

Chelsfield Church – The Church of St Martin of Tours dates mainly from the 13th century. Detached from the village, it has a pleasant rural setting and won a borough 'Greenest Church' award in 1994-5.

REFRESHMENTS:
The Five Bells, Chelsfield.
The Kent Hounds, Well Hill.

Walk 15   HAINAULT FOREST   3¹/₄m (5¹/₄km)

Maps: OS Sheets Landranger 177; Pathfinder 1141.

A walk along forest trails within a Country Park.

Start: At 476926, the main car park, Hainault Forest Country Park.

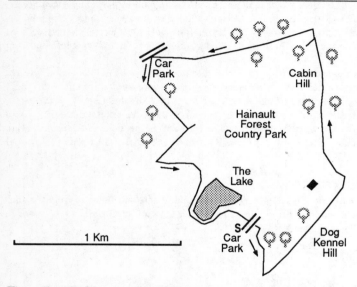

The walk starts from the refreshment kiosk next to the car park.

Walk up the hill immediately behind the kiosk, keeping the trees to your left and a large open field to the right. After about 400 yards a track can be seen just in the trees, with a golf course beyond. Turn left along this track, which gradually ascends Dog Kennel Hill. At a crossing path next to a wooden gate, keep ahead, with the wooden stake fence and the golf course still on your right.

Soon the track curves left around an animal enclosure to reach Fox Burrow Road near a row of cottages: cross and continue along a gravel track up Cabin Hill. At the summit, keep ahead past an information board. From this point, take the second track on the left (about 50 yards after the information board), following it eastwards through the trees and then across an open field. Now head for the car park next to Lambourn Road. (The Two Brewers Inn is about 200 yards to the left along the road from the car park).

From the car park turn left along the waymarked track, following it back into the forest, ignoring smaller paths to both the left and the right. After about $1/4$ mile the track meets another, major, track near some wooden barriers: turn right along this broad gravel track which is part of the Three Forests Way. After about 400 yards, turn sharp left along another gravel track. At the next crossing of paths, in a small clearing, keep right along the main track. Where this forks, go right and walk around the northern end of the lake, continuing back to the car park.

POINTS OF INTEREST:
Hainault Forest Country Park – The park consists of approximately 1000 acres of forest and common land. There is a lake near the main car park, a number of waymarked woodland trails and an animal enclosure. The woodlands were once part of the great Royal Forest of Essex.

REFRESHMENTS:
The Two Brewers, Lambourne Road.

Walk 16   BAKER STREET AND MARYLEBONE   3¹/₄m (5¹/₄km)

Maps: OS Sheets Landranger 176; Pathfinder 1159.
A busy street circuit.
Start: At 279820, Baker Street Underground Station.

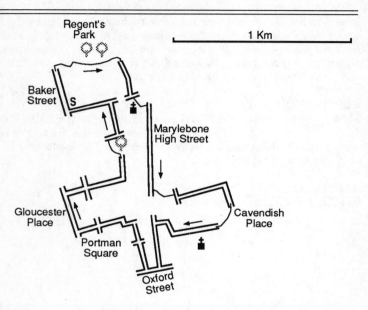

It is difficult to walk around the Baker Street area without coming across images of Sherlock Holmes: his silhouette even adorns the walls of the Tube Station! Leave by the Baker Street (North) exit and turn right to walk to the Regent's Park end of the street, passing the **Sherlock Holmes Museum** (on the other side of the street) along the way. At the end, turn right to enter the park at Clarence Gate. Go right for a short distance and then cross a footbridge. At the end of the bridge turn right.

At York Bridge Road, turn right to go back across the water. Now leave the park at York Gate and keep ahead towards St Marylebone Parish Church. Walk to the left of the church and go left from the east door to reach Marylebone High Street. Turn right and walk along the High Street, passing a Memorial Garden. After about ¹/₃ mile, just before the Angel Inn, bear left into Marylebone Lane. Follow this around to the right, and then go left into Bulstrode Street. At the end, turn right and almost immediately left into Queen Anne Street. Cross Wimpole Street and Harley Street, and at the end keep right along Chandos Street. Go over Cavendish Place and then walk diagonally across Cavendish Square Gardens. Go past the former home of Herbert Asquith, along Henrietta Place.

The road passes the rear of several Oxford Street stores and St Peter's Church: at the end, go right along Marylebone Lane and then turn left at the lights into Wigmore Street. At the next set of lights, turn left into James Street: this street contains many restaurants and on summer evenings, with customers wining and dining at tables on the pavement, the area has a 'continental' atmosphere. Upon reaching the junction with Oxford Street, turn right and, just before Selfridges, go right again along Duke Street. Keep ahead to reach Manchester Square, leaving the square by going left down Fitzhardinge Street. Cross Baker Street and walk along the northern edge of Portman Square, turning right into Gloucester Place. Turn right again at Blandford Street and, with Telecom Tower ahead, cross Baker Street once more. Walk past the Lincoln Inn and then turn left into Aybrook Street. At the end, go left into **Paddington Street Gardens**. Go right, then leave by the right-hand gate at Paddington Street. Cross and walk along Luxborough Street. At the end, opposite Madam Tussaud's and the London Planetarium, turn left and walk past the University of Westminster Campus. Now cross at the lights to reach an entrance to Baker Street Station.

POINTS OF INTEREST:

Sherlock Holmes Museum – Close to the Volunteer Inn, the Museum has a door numbered 221b, the address of Conan Doyle's fictitious detective. The building is actually 239 Baker Street and includes Hudson's Old English restaurant as well as rooms recreated in the style that Holmes might have had them.

Paddington Street Gardens – There are two sections of gardens either side of Paddington Street. This site was used as a burial ground during the 18th century. It is estimated that there are around 80,000 graves here and although the garden is now a recreation area it is still consecrated ground. A mausoleum stands in the south garden and there is a charming statue of a 'Street Orderly Boy' by Donato Barcaglia.

REFRESHMENTS:

The Volunteer Inn, Baker Street.
The Christi Ristorante Italiano, James Street.

Walk 17   ALDENHAM COUNTRY PARK $3\frac{1}{4}$m ($5\frac{1}{4}$km)

Maps: OS Sheets Landranger 176; Pathfinder 1139.
A Country Park and reservoir circuit.
Start: At 178953, crossroads in Elstree village.

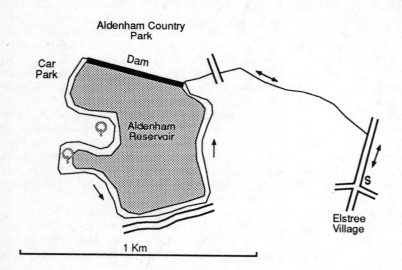

Walk up **Elstree** High Street past the Plough Inn and the Parish Church. After the Hollybush Inn, go left over a stile at a double public footpath sign. Walk diagonally down the hill on the grass, then go through two metal kissing gates and across a meadow to reach a stile. Go over on to a minor road. Cross the road and walk forward along a tarmac drive into **Aldenham Country Park**. Go to the right of a wooden gate and through a car parking area towards the reservoir.

Turn right and walk along the dam on the northern edge of the reservoir. At the end of the dam, turn left to walk between the reservoir and the car park: there is a picnic area nearby. At the end of the car park, keep ahead through a wooden gate to reach an animal area and playground. Turn left at the adventure playground and walk between the wooden posts to reach a footpath.

40

Follow a section of this tree-lined nature trail around the edges of the reservoir. At marker post Number 2, just past a wooden sculpture, bear right. Now from the signpost, go left to continue the lakeside walk in the direction of Watford Road, walking alongside the South Bay Wildlife Refuge and between the reservoir and the road. Shortly after passing the Fishery Inn, follow the path to the left, passing the sailing club to reach the Anglers' Car Park, completing a full circuit of the reservoir.

To return to start, reverse the outward route to Elstree village.

POINTS OF INTEREST:

Elstree – The village seems to have been divided into quarters by the roads running through it, but there are a number of buildings of interest including the Parish Church. The famous Elstree Film Studios are about $1^1/_2$ miles west of the village, at Borehamwood.

Aldenham Country Park – The Park based around the reservoir contains a nature trail, guided walks, picnic areas and an adventure playground. The reservoir dam was built by French prisoners of war in about 1795 with a major reconstruction carried out in 1976/7.

REFRESHMENTS:

The Plough, Elstree High Street.

Walkers wanting to take their own refreshments should make for the Picnic Area in Aldenham Country Park.

THE EAST END $3^1/_2$m ($5^1/_2$km)
or 6m ($9^1/_2$km)

Maps: OS Sheets Landranger 177; Pathfinder 1159.
A walk through diverse East End streets.
Start: At 333816, Liverpool Street Station.

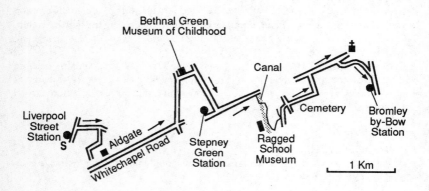

The phrase 'East End' conjures up a number of images and this walk provides a sample of the various dimensions of this historic part of London. The shorter walk ends at Stepney Green Tube Station, the longer route continues to Bromley-by-Bow.

Leave Liverpool Street Station by the Bishopsgate exit. Turn left into Bishopsgate and, after about 200 yards, turn right into Brushfield Street. Walk past Spitalfields Market, and when you are opposite Christ Church and The Ten Bells Inn (formerly the Jack the Ripper), turn right into Commercial Street. After about 50 yards, where Commercial Street bears left, continue down Toynbee Street. At the end, turn right and go along Wentworth Street to Middlesex Street, home of Petticoat Lane Market. Turn left, and at the end follow the pavement around to the right. Go under Houndsditch by means of subway exit 4. Leave by exit 1 and turn right along St James's Passage. Go left at Mitre Street and left again into Aldgate and Aldgate High Street, passing St Botolph's Church and Aldgate Station. Continue via subway exit 13. Leave by exit 15 and turn left into Whitechapel High Street. Continue for nearly a mile, then, at the traffic lights next to the Blind Beggar, turn left. Cross Cambridge Heath Road and follow it until you pass under the railway bridge and Bethnal Green Gardens (initially a concrete playground) appears on the right. Now walk through the Gardens on the path close to the road. Go through two iron gates and cross Roman Road. Go past St John's Church to reach the **Museum of Childhood**. From the Museum exit, go left down Museum Passage. At the end, cross and continue on Sugar Loaf Walk. At the Camel Inn, turn right and walk down Globe Road. Cross Roman Road and continue under the railway bridge and on to the Old Globe Inn. Stepney Green Station, the finish for the shorter version of the walk is to the right.

The longer version of the walk continues by turning left into Mile End Road, passing the buildings of Queen Mary College. At the sign, on the right, to the Ragged School Museum, cross the road and go down Grand Walk, next to the canal. Cross the bridge at Solebay Street and turn right along the pavement. Follow Copperfield Road to reach the **Ragged School Museum**. Turn left down Rhodeswell Road, and immediately left again through a gate into Mile End Park. Take the first path on the right, going past the northern end of the athletics track. Continue for a short way on the cobbled road, then turn left. Cross Burdett Road and go ahead down Eric Street. At the second crossroads, turn right into Hamlets Way. Follow this as it becomes pedestrianised, with a cemetery to the right. Pass two tower blocks, then turn left into Wellington Way. Go right at the end to pass Bow Road Underground Station. Now follow Bow Road towards St Mary's Church. Turn right down Bromley High Street (level with the statue of Gladstone), following it around to the left. At the junction, turn right into St Leonard's Street to reach Bromley-by-Bow Underground Station.

POINTS OF INTEREST:

Bethnal Green Museum of Childhood – The upper galleries contain displays relating to the history of childhood. The lower floor houses one of the largest collections of toys on public display in the world, including a collection of pre-1930 teddy bears.
The Ragged School Museum – This was one of the original schools set up by Dr Barnardo. On certain days the Museum is open to the public.

REFRESHMENTS:

The Old Globe, Stepney Green.
There are also other possibilities, as mentioned in the route description.

Walk 20   KINGSTON-UPON-THAMES   3½m (5½km)

Maps: OS Sheets Landranger 176; Pathfinder 1174 and 1190.
A fine town and towpath walk.
Start: At 182695, Kingston Railway Station.

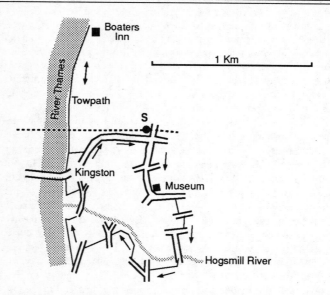

Leave the Station by the main entrance and cross at the lights. Walk down Clarence Street (with the Bus Station on the other side), and, at the next lights, continue along Wheatfield Way, crossing over to reach **Kingston Museum**.

From the Museum exit, turn left and then left again down Fairfield Road. Upon reaching the Albion Tavern, turn right and cross Fairfield Recreation Ground along the tree-lined path. At the far side, go over the pedestrian crossing and turn left. Immediately after the Cricketers Inn, turn right along a paved footpath called 'Millfield'. Walk through the visitors parking area and then turn right along pedestrianised Mill Place. At the end, turn left, passing the curiously-named Cocoanut Inn. After passing numerous attractive cottages and yet another inn, you will reach a small footbridge. Cross and go right along a footpath. Shortly after crossing the Hogsmill River by means of a larger footbridge, go right through a gate in the fence.

Follow the path beside the river to the road. Now do not go over the Knights Park Bridge: instead, turn left, and then right down Denmark Road. After about 200 yards, at Heron Court, turn right along the Hogsmill Walk. Despite the urban surroundings, heron have been known to fish on this stretch of river.

Cross the dual carriageway and continue along Oaklea Passage. At the end of the passage, turn right and then left down South Lane. This lane joins the main road where Portsmouth Road meets Kingston High Street: cross and turn right along the riverside path, heading for Kingston Bridge. At the Waters Edge Bar, turn right and walk past the craft shops (the detour is necessary because of private land immediately next to the river). Turn left at the High Street and cross the **Clattern Bridge**.

Shortly the High Street leads into Market Place where there are numerous attractive buildings: after passing Woolworths, turn left into a passageway signposted 'Riverside'. This emerges at the Gazebo Inn: turn right and walk under Kingston Bridge and the railway bridge. Now follow the towpath as far as the Boaters Inn (Teddington Lock is just over a mile further on if you feel like continuing along the towpath). To complete the route, turn back from the Boaters Inn reversing the walk along the towpath to return to the town. Go under the railway bridge and past the Sea Cadet Corps building and then follow the road left at the Outrigger Inn. Continue forward along the side road, with the multi-storey car park on your left. At the main road (opposite Bentalls) turn left. Cross at the traffic lights and head up the raised walkway to return to the railway station.

POINTS OF INTEREST:

Kingston Museum – The Museum is well worth visiting if you wish to find out more about this famous royal borough. The dignified red-brick buildings contain local history exhibitions, an art gallery and a gift shop. The Museum is closed on Wednesdays and Sundays.

Clattern Bridge – This bridge across the Hogsmill River, a tributary of the Thames, dates from at least 1293. It is believed to have taken its name from the clattering of horses crossing the river in medieval times. The Coronation Stone, another ancient monument, and the Town Hall, a more modern edifice, are nearby. According to tradition, seven Saxon Kings were crowned in Kingston.

REFRESHMENTS:

The Gazebo, Kingston Riverside.
The Boaters Inn, Kingston Riverside.
Several other good inns are mentioned in the route description.

Walk 21   WHITEHALL AND WESTMINSTER $3\frac{1}{2}$m ($5\frac{1}{2}$km)

Maps: OS Sheets Landranger 176 and 177; Pathfinder 1175 and 1159.

A short Central London street walk.

Start: At 304804, Embankment Underground Station.

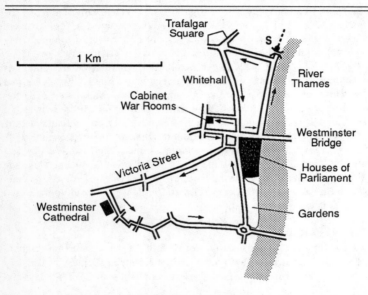

Leave the station by the Villiers Street/Charing Cross exit and go under the railway bridge through Embankment Place. Turn right and walk along Northumberland Avenue. On reaching Trafalgar Square, cross over at the lights and go down Whitehall (first left from Northumberland Avenue).

Walking down Whitehall you will pass the buildings of many major government departments including the Ministry of Defence, the Cabinet Office, the Foreign Office and the Treasury. Cross Whitehall to view Downing Street, complete with security gates.

After passing the Cenotaph, turn right down King Charles Street. Go down the steps at the end of the street and pass the entrance to the **Cabinet War Rooms**. Now go left along Horse Guards Road which is next to St James's Park. Turn left again down Great George Street and, at the lights, cross over to go along the western edge of Parliament Square, where statues of many famous political figures can be seen, including George Canning and Abraham Lincoln. This is also the point at which to view St Margaret's Church and Westminster Abbey.

From the Abbey, head away from Parliament Square up Victoria Street for about ³/₄ mile, passing many shops and the huge Westminster City Hall, to reach the piazza of **Westminster Cathedral**. Walk to the left of the Cathedral, along Ambrosden Avenue. At the end, cross the road and continue ahead down an alleyway called 'Windsor Place' (next to The Cardinal Inn). At Greencoat Place, turn left, then right down Emery Hill Street. Cross Rochester Row and go down Vincent Square, passing some of the buildings of Westminster College and the Royal Horticultural Society Hall. Turn left down Elverton Street and right along Horseferry Road, following this to reach the roundabout at Lambeth Bridge.

Cross using the pedestrian crossing and enter Victoria Tower Gardens via the steps next to the bridge. Note the view of Lambeth Palace across the river. Walk through the gardens, pausing to admire the *Burghers of Calais* by Auguste Rodin and a statue of Emmeline Pankhurst. Turn right along Abingdon Street, leading to Parliament Square, with the English Heritage's Jewel Tower on your left and the Houses of Parliament prominent to the right.

At the corner of the Square, turn right along Bridge Street. A short detour over Westminster Bridge is worthwhile for the traditional view of the Houses of Parliament from the South Bank. Retrace your steps over the bridge. Westminster Station is nearby for a return by Underground, but the walk along Victoria Embankment adds less than ¹/₂ mile on the return to Embankment Station.

POINTS OF INTEREST:
The Cabinet War Rooms – This was the underground headquarters of British Government during the Second World War. Churchill made many of his war plans here.
Westminster Cathedral – This Roman Catholic Cathedral, built in a Byzantine style, was consecrated in 1903. It has the widest nave in England and is 284 feet high.

REFRESHMENTS:
The Sherlock Holmes, Northumberland Street.
There are also many other possibilities along the route.

Walk 22   REGENT'S PARK   3½m (5½km)

Maps: OS Sheets Landranger 176; Pathfinder 1159.
Easy and scenic parkland walking.
Start: At 287822, Regent's Park Underground Station.

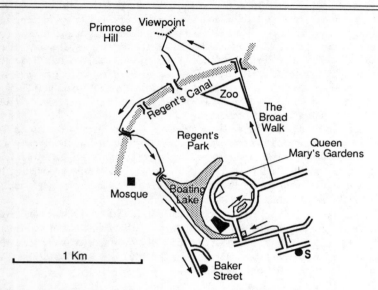

The Regent's Park area provides elegant and interesting settings for walkers in the heart of London. The Park was the idea of the Prince Regent, later to become George IV. Much of the design was by John Nash.

From the station exit, turn left and walk to the traffic lights. Cross over and continue down Park Square West. Go across the Outer Circle and enter Regent's Park through the gate directly ahead. Almost immediately, turn left and walk along the tarmac path to a road. At the road, turn right and walk across York Bridge. Continue ahead, with Regent's College on the left, crossing the Inner Circle and reaching the main entrance gate to Queen Mary's Gardens.

From the gate the Triton Fountain and the Open Air Theatre (ahead and to the left) can be seen. However, do not take the broad path in this direction: instead, take the first path to the right and walk to the left of a lake, crossing a small wooden bridge with a cascade to the left. Pause to admire the Bronze Eagle Statue in the water, then continue around the northern edge of the lake, passing another statue, this one representing the Mighty Hunter. After passing this, turn left along the path through the centre of the Rose Garden.

Leave through the gate and continue along the left-hand side of Chester Road to reach a green gate. Turn left and walk along The Broad Walk, passing the Tea House and a fountain before reaching the perimeter fence of London Zoo.

Continue past the zoo, crossing the Outer Circle once more. Now cross St Mark's Bridge over Regent's Canal and turn left down Prince Albert Road. Cross at the next set of traffic lights to enter **Primrose Hill**, taking the right-hand path up the hill. From the top of the hill there are superb views across London.

Continue over the hill, then follow the path leftwards to reach the southern corner of Primrose Hill and the gate to Prince Albert Road: the Telecom Tower can be seen ahead. Cross the pedestrian crossing, go right for a short distance and then turn left where there is a sign indicating 'Canal Side Walk'. Turn right along the path before the bridge, then go right along the towpath (which connects Camden Lock to Little Venice), passing under a road bridge.

Walk up the path to the right just before the second bridge, then cross the footbridge and the Outer Circle to re-enter Regent's Park. Fork right, then right again after about 100 yards. At the refreshment kiosk and public conveniences, turn right to cross the bridge over Hanover Island. Now, as the London Central Mosque comes into view, turn left to walk by the side of the **Boating Lake**. Keep on the lakeside path until, after about 500 yards, Clarence Gate can be seen to the right. Go through the gate, cross the Outer Circle road, going briefly right and then left to head down Baker Street. The Underground Station entrance is about 200 yards down Baker Street, on the left.

POINTS OF INTEREST:

Primrose Hill – From the viewpoint at the top of this famous, grassy 206-foot hill a superb panorama of London opens out.

Boating Lake – The lake provides a home for around 90 species of waterfowl and is an official inland bird observatory. Herons breed on one of the islands.

REFRESHMENTS:

The Broad Walk Tea House, Regent's Park.

Walk 23 HOLLAND PARK AND KENSINGTON 3½m (5½km)

Maps: OS Sheets Landranger 176; Pathfinder 1159 and 1175.
Busy West London streets and parks.
Start: At 232800, Shepherd's Bush Underground Station.

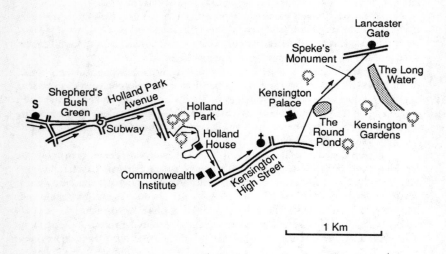

From Shepherd's Bush Station, turn left along the Uxbridge Road, walking as far as the main traffic lights. Go across and then right to reach Shepherd's Bush Common. Follow the footpath around the western and southern edges of this triangular green. Towards the end of the green cross the road (Shepherd's Bush Green) opposite Rockley Road and a car park.

Turn left to continue along Shepherd's Bush Green, going under a bridge cunningly disguised as a high-speed train! Continue through the second subway, turning left at its end to reach Holland Park Avenue. Walk along Holland Park Avenue for about ⅓ mile until a road called Holland Park appears on the right.

Walk along Holland Park for approximately 400 yards, passing Holland Park Mews, and continuing into Abbotsbury Road to reach a small gate, on the left, into **Holland Park** itself. Go through the gate, turn right, and then take the first path on

50

the left, a tree-lined gravel path, known as Chestnut Walk, going slightly uphill. As you reach the top of the hill there is a pond and a wildlife reserve on your left and two paths to the right: take the second of these paths and walk past the statue of Lord Holland to reach a T-junction at the eastern edge of the Park. Here, turn right and walk downhill along the tarmac path towards Holland House, turning right along the path signposted to the 'Kyoto Garden'.

After passing Holland House, take the path on the left (signposted to 'The Orangery') and then go right to walk through the terraced garden (there is a cafeteria next to this garden). At the end of the garden, where there is a row of wooden benches, turn left. Do not leave the park yet: instead, continue leftwards, passing a children's play area to reach a gate. Go through and follow the path to the left, going around the fenced cricket pitch. Keep to the fence as it passes the rear of Holland House and then curves right towards Kensington High Street. The buildings of the **Commonwealth Institute** can be seen ahead, and there is an entrance on the right.

Continue along the path out of Holland Park to reach Kensington High Street. Here, turn left and walk along the High Street, with its many interesting shops, for about $^1/_3$ mile to reach Kensington Gardens, on the left.

Go through the first gate into Kensington Gardens and walk forwards along the path, with Kensington Palace on the left, to reach a signpost. Cross 'The Broad Walk' and then bear half-left, heading for the Round Pond. Go to the left-hand side of the pond and, after about 100 yards, take the second diagonal path on the left. Follow this path for approximately $^1/_2$ mile, passing Speke's Monument, to reach the Westbourne Gate. Now cross Bayswater to reach Lancaster Gate Station from where the start of the walk is regained by underground train.

POINTS OF INTEREST:

Holland Park – Formerly a private garden, this 55 acre park includes a Dutch garden and reputedly contains the nearest woodland to central London. Holland House, a Jacobean mansion, was badly damaged during the Second World War: the restored east wing now incorporates a youth hostel.

Commonwealth Institute – Opened in 1962, the Institute contains a Library, Shop, Brasserie, Conference and Events Centre and Exhibition Galleries relating to Commonwealth countries. A high-tech, interactive, educational exhibition entitled 'Wonders of the World' is due to open in mid-1996.

REFRESHMENTS:

The walker should have no problem finding refreshments on this route. Shepherd's Bush and Kensington provide a host of eating and drinking venues.

CHIGWELL $3^1/_2$m ($5^1/_2$km)
or $6^1/_4$m (10km)

Maps: OS Sheets Landranger 177; Pathfinder 1141.
Undulating country lanes and footpaths.
Start: At 450926, Grange Hill Underground Station.

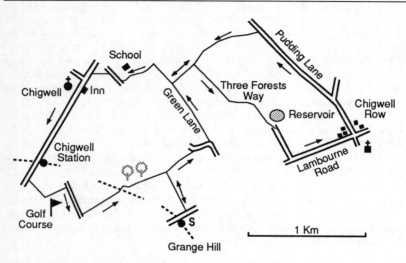

From the station exit, cross the road and turn right. Walk past the garden centre and
turn left along a signposted footpath. After about $^1/_4$ mile this reaches a junction of
paths at a 'Chigwell Country Walk' signpost: take the right-hand path and walk along
field edges to reach a road, emerging between two cottages. Cross and go right. At
the next bend, turn left along a tarmac bridleway called 'Green Lane'. Go past two
cottages, beyond which the track then becomes a true green lane, typical of this part
of Essex. After about $^1/_3$ mile you will reach a junction with a permissive path to
Pudding Lane.

    The shorter walk continues ahead here, the longer route rejoining at this point
after making a circuit to the east.

    The longer route turns right along the permissive path to reach the corner at the
end of the first field. Here, follow the track to the right, with a hedgerow on your left:
this track is part of the Three Forests Way. At the next field corner, keep ahead and

uphill, as indicated by the marker post. At the next post the path bears half-left across a field: this path can be overgrown in the summer so take care not to miss it. At the end, turn right and walk beside the railings of a reservoir site to reach a gate. Go through and ahead along the drive beyond, continuing to Grove Lane with its weatherboarded cottages. At the end, turn left and walk along Lambourne Road for $^1/_3$ mile to reach the Chigwell Row crossroads. Turn left and go down Gravel Lane. At the bottom of the hill, fork left along Pudding Lane, following it for $^1/_2$ mile until, after passing a number of houses, a signposted path to Chigwell is reached on the left. Ignore a stile to the left and keep ahead along the field edge: there are good views of Epping Forest on the horizon. Go over the next stile and continue downhill. At the bottom, you are back at the junction with the Three Forests Way passed earlier. Keep forward to regain Green Lane once more and turn right to rejoin the shorter route.

Walk up the hill for about 300 yards until a Chigwell Country Walk sign can be seen on the left. Turn left as indicated, following the path as it winds around to eventually emerge at a gate by a road. Cross and go over the stile slightly to the right. Follow the footpath beyond to reach **Chigwell**'s main street, opposite the school. Turn left and walk between Ye Olde Kings Head Inn and St Mary's Church. Continue downhill for $^1/_2$ mile to reach Chigwell Station, continue past the garden centre and along the road's grass verge for about 200 yards before turning left along a signposted footpath next to a hedge. The path runs next to, and across, a golf course: at Hainault Road, cross and turn right. Walk gently uphill for 300 yards to reach a signed footpath on the left, next to a bus stop. Go along this to reach a road. Go straight ahead along the left-hand side of Broadhurst Gardens, then keep ahead along the cycle path. Cross the next road and maintain direction along a gravel path. Cross the railway and immediately turn right at a junction of paths. At the corner of the field the path bears right temporarily and then follows the course indicated by the yellow arrows, going along the field edge. At the next corner there is a T-junction: turn right and follow the footpath back to Manor Road and Grange Hill station.

POINTS OF INTEREST:

Chigwell – The three focal points of this Essex village are Chigwell School, St Mary's Church and Ye Olde Kings Head Inn. The inn is said to have been used by Dickens as inspiration for 'The Maypole' in *Barnaby Rudge*. Confusingly, there is now a real 'Maypole' in Chigwell Row!

REFRESHMENTS:

Ye Olde Kings Head Inn, Chigwell Row.

Walk 26 HORSENDEN HILL $3^1/_2$m ($5^1/_2$km)

Maps: OS Sheets Landranger 176; Pathfinder 1158.

A canal towpath and a moderate hill.

Start: At 180838, Alperton Underground Station.

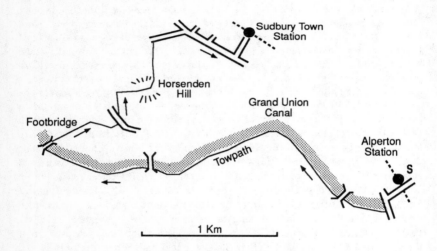

This relatively easy walk takes in a stretch of the Grand Union Canal and finishes with a climb over Horsenden Hill. It starts from Alperton Tube Station and finishes at Sudbury Town, one stop further along the Piccadilly line.

From Alperton Station, cross the road and turn right. At the junction of Ealing Road and Bridgewater Road bear left along the pavement and, after about 30 yards, go left down the steps to reach the Grand Union Canal. Turn left to join the westward bound towpath.

Keep on the towpath for about two miles, going past a supermarket complex, under a road bridge and into less urban terrain with back gardens on your side of the canal and a golf course on the far side. There is a straight section of canal followed by several bends, the towpath then passes under another road bridge and, after a further $^1/_2$ mile, reaches a footbridge.

Cross the footbridge to view an information board relating to **Horsenden Hill**. Now turn left and walk along the path to the right of a number of rugby fields, heading towards the hill. Just after the last rugby pitch the grass path you are following forks, next to a gap in the hedgerow. Take the right branch, going through the gap in the hedge and then immediately taking the left-hand grass path towards the corner of the field. Go between the trees at the corner and then ahead along the well-defined grass track going uphill. At the far corner of the field, turn left along a smaller footpath, going between trees to reach a road.

Cross the road carefully and follow another small footpath opposite. This path links immediately to a tarmac footpath: turn left along this, but when it reaches a red brick public convenience building, turn right along the grass track leading to the summit of the hill. There is a green plateau at the top, with a triangulation point marking the summit.

When you have finished admiring the views, continue ahead, going down on the grass track. As you approach the trees this track divides into two: take the left branch through the woods, not the one passing close to the golf course. Keep along the main path, going downhill through the centre of this wooded section of the walk to reach, after about $1/_4$ mile, a set of barriers next to the end of a road. Turn right and walk along the road for about 250 yards to reach a T-junction. Turn right, following the sign for Sudbury Town Underground Station which is reached by turning left down Crossgate.

POINTS OF INTEREST:
Horsenden Hill – The hill provides fine views across several parts of London: Sudbury and Harrow are north and Northolt is to the west. The variety of natural habitats around the hill support a range of plants and animals.

REFRESHMENTS:
The Pleasure Boat, Alperton.

Walk 27   PYMME'S BROOK   3³/₄m (6km)

Maps: OS Sheets Landranger 176; Pathfinder 1140.

A walk through parks and along a riverside trail.

Start: At 309927, Palmers Green Railway Station.

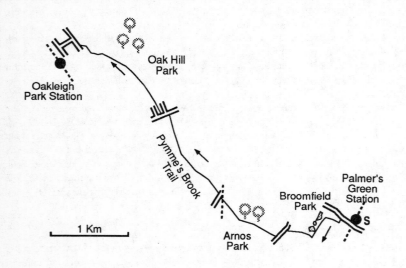

The route includes a number of parks and about 2¹/₂ miles of the Pymme's Brook Trail which is indicated by blue and white circular symbols. It finishes at Oakleigh Park Station, from where it is possible to catch a train back to Palmers Green via Alexandra Palace.

From the station, cross, turn right and walk along Alderman's Hill. After about 200 yards, turn left through an entrance to Broomfield Park. Walk along the path by the fence, as indicated by the **Pymme's Brook Trail** marker. When you reach blue and white gates, turn left and walk past a pond to reach a T-junction of paths. Turn right, and then left to walk between a further series of ponds and **Broomfield House**. At the end of the ponds, turn right and walk under the walled archway. Now follow the path along the southern edge of the park, leaving through the gate at the corner.

Cross the road and turn left down Wilmer Way. Cross Morton Way and turn right through the wooden gate opposite Ashridge Gardens to enter Arnos Park. Bear left along the concrete path: Pymme's Brook and a series of weeping willow trees are to the left.

The route now follows the course of Pymme's Brook for about $2^1/_2$ miles, a very pleasant green route through a suburban part of London. Keep to the right of the brook in the park and, at the next gate, cross the road, passing under the railway bridge at the same time.

The tarmac path again keeps to the right of the brook as it makes its way through an area known as 'Waterfall Walk'. Cross Osidge Lane, turn left and then right down East Walk. Keep to the right of the brook again, this time on the grass. At the end of this section, follow the brook into Oak Hill Park, passing to the left of a car park. Towards the end of Oak Hill Park there is a T-junction of tarmac paths: turn left over a bridge and then immediately right, leaving the Pymme's Brook Trail at this point. Walk along a path for about 300 yards, ignoring a left fork, but turning left at the next path to reach Church Hill Road. Cross and turn right. After about 200 yards, turn left along Capel Road. At the end, go left along Alverstone Avenue and then, shortly, turn right over a footbridge to reach Oakleigh Park Station. From here there are fairly frequent trains to Alexandra Palace.

POINTS OF INTEREST:

Pymme's Brook Trail – This is a 10 mile trail through the parks and open spaces of North London. The section covered in this walk includes Broomfield Park, Arnos Park and Oak Hill Park with their various sports and recreational facilties. The latter park contains a nature reserve.

Broomfield House – Parts of this Grade II listed building date from the 16th century. The House was badly damaged by fire in 1984 and 1993, but Enfield Council hope to restore it to its original condition and character.

REFRESHMENTS: There are shops and cafes near Palmers Green Station and at East Barnet near the finish of the walk.

Walk 28   **PARKLAND WALK**   3¾m (6km)

Maps: OS Sheets Landranger 176; Pathfinder 1159.

A walk along a disused railway track and through woodland.

Start: At 314868, Finsbury Park Station.

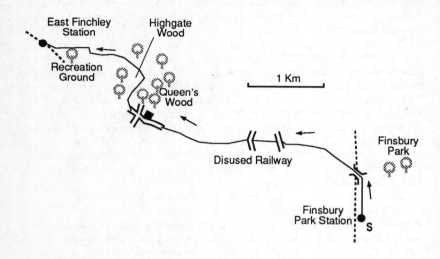

From the main station exit, turn left into Station Place. Immediately cross Stroud Green Road (close to the railway bridge) and go through a walled entrance on to the Parkland Walk footpath. This path winds along between the railway, on the left, and **Finsbury Park**, on the right. When you reach the Oxford Road Gate (Finsbury Park cafeteria can be seen to the right), turn left and go over the railway bridge.

At the end of the bridge, turn right to continue along the Parkland Walk, which now follows a disused railway track connecting Finsbury Park to Highgate Wood. The track provides a precious 'green lane' and a refuge for wildlife in the heart of North London: follow it for about two miles.

The walk passes over Stapleton Hall Road, under Crouch Hill and between former station platforms. About a mile later, just before two tunnels, the walker must leave the Parkland Walkway. Proceed up Holmesdale Road and then turn right along busy

Archway Road, passing Highgate Underground Station. Walk past the Woodman Inn and over the Muswell Hill Road. After passing Highgate Police Station (across the road), turn right to enter **Highgate Wood** via Archway Gate.

Now go forward along the tarmac path for about 400 yards to reach the Lodge Gate Entrance. At the crossing of gravel paths close to the gate, turn left and walk to the right of The Lodge. Follow the tarmac/stone path to pass the Drinking Fountain, continuing to reach the Bridge Gate Exit.

Go through the gate and continue along the path to reach Lanchester Road. Turn right, then cross Woodside Avenue and go along Fordington Road. Where this turns left, continue ahead, going through a gate into Cherry Tree Wood Recreation Ground. Walk along the path to the far corner, nearest the railway: East Finchley Underground Station is just across the road and from it trains run back to the start.

POINTS OF INTEREST:

Finsbury Park – Anyone with surplus energy may wish to detour to explore this popular recreational area. Opened in 1869 it was one of London's first municipal parks.

Highgate Wood – Despite their urban setting, these woods are relatively unspoilt and provide an interesting diversion from the busy surrounding roads. The woods were once part of the Great Forest of Middlesex.

REFRESHMENTS:

The Woodman Inn, Highgate.
Finsbury Park Cafeteria.

Walk 29   SYDENHAM HILL AND DULWICH   3³/₄m (6km)

Maps: OS Sheets Landranger 176 or 177; Pathfinder 1175.
An easy stroll through woods and parks.
Start: At 336721, Sydenham Hill Railway Station.

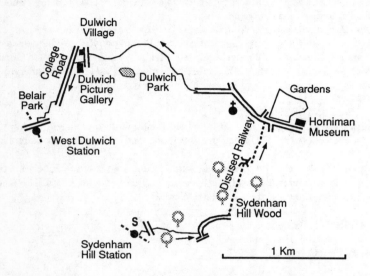

There are trains from Victoria to Sydenham Hill. The walk finishes at West Dulwich station which is also on the line to Victoria.

Use the longer walkway and steps to reach College Road. Go directly across the road and through a white gate on to a broad, tree-lined path. Walk uphill, with Dulwich Woods on the left. Keep on the tarmac drive to reach a gate at the top of the hill, opposite the Dulwich Wood House Inn. Beyond the gate, turn left along Crescent Wood Road. After about ¼ mile there is an entrance to **Sydenham Hill Wood** Nature Reserve on the left: walk down the sloping footpath and bear left at the information board to join a path that takes you over a tunnel entrance. Next, join the disused railway track, heading north away from Crescent Wood Tunnel. After about ¼ mile on the disused railway, just before a low wooden bench, bear left up a set of steps constructed from trees. Follow the path ahead through the wood to reach a green metal gate. Go through, cross a footbridge and fork left. Now go left again, at a lamp-post, along a smaller footpath. Stay on this path as it goes downhill, passing a number of blocks of flats. As the path levels out, maintain direction along a pavement and then a tarmac path which leads between fences to reach a main road. Cross Sydenham Hill and Lordship Lane at the lights to reach the entrance to Horniman Gardens. Keep left, taking the tarmac path along the western edge of the park. Towards the corner, follow the path on the right, going uphill. Keep on this path to pass a number of animal pens and a bandstand. Continue along the main, tree-lined drive to leave the gardens. At the road, turn left to reach the entrance to the **Horniman Museum**.

Upon leaving the Museum, turn right and walk along Lordship Lane, passing the Horniman Gardens once more. Cross Lordship Lane at the traffic lights close to St Peter's Church and turn left down the road called 'Dulwich Common'. Shortly after the Lordship Lane Estate, turn right through the main entrance to Dulwich Park. Fork left on the broad entrance drive, passing a lodge. Almost immediately, turn right along a smaller tarmac drive, and then walk left around the circular area. Stay on the path until it joins a main drive through the park, then bear left on this. Now, at the triangular section, bear left again towards Old College Gate (the cafe, tennis courts and boating lake are to the left). At the gate, cross, turn left and walk along College Road for about 50 yards to reach the entrance to the **Dulwich Picture Gallery**. Leave the Gallery by the gate at the northern end of the building and go left along Gallery Road for about $\frac{1}{4}$ mile. Turn right at a gated entrance into Belair Park. Walk to the left of the main building and then go left again to pass the public conveniences. The path takes you around the southern end of the park and reaches a car park and tennis courts: turn right and then go left at the end of the tennis courts to reach a gate at Thurlow Park Road, and West Dulwich Station.

POINTS OF INTEREST:

Sydenham Hill Wood – This 9 hectare Nature Reserve is maintained by the London Wildlife Trust. Together with Dulwich Wood it forms one of the largest woodland areas in South London.

Horniman Museum – The museum contains the rather bizarre and diverse collection of exhibits assembled by Frederick Horniman.

Dulwich Picture Gallery – The Gallery houses the works of many distinguished artists and claims to be the oldest art gallery in the country.

REFRESHMENTS:

Dulwich Wood House, Sydenham Hill.

Walk 30   THE SOUTH BANK   4m (6½km)

Maps: OS Sheets Landranger 177; Pathfinder 1159 and 1175.
A riverside walk from Lambeth to the Tower.
Start: At 312799, Waterloo Station.

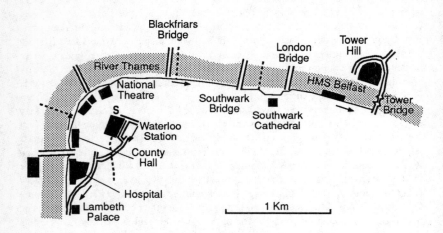

Leave Waterloo Station by the main exit/entrance facing Waterloo Road. Turn right and right again to go along the south-eastern side of the station building. Go down the steps and turn left along the subway to reach Lower Marsh. Turn right, cross the main road at the traffic lights, and continue ahead along Upper Marsh, looking behind for a view of the Waterloo International train terminal.

Turn left along Lambeth Palace Road, crossing at the lights opposite St Thomas's Hospital Accident and Emergency Unit. Continue along Lambeth Palace Road until the Palace itself appears on the left. Now turn right along the riverside walk. The route now keeps as close as possible to the south bank of the Thames until Tower Bridge is reached. Admire the view of the Houses of Parliament on the other side of the river and follow the Silver Jubilee Walkway indicators. Cross the Westminster Bridge road and continue along the river walk, passing County Hall, 'The home of

London Government from 1922 to 1986', and Jubilee Gardens. Next the concrete buildings of the South Bank complex appear. These include the Royal Festival Hall, the **Museum of the Moving Image**, the National Film Theatre and the National Theatre.

Continue past Gabriel's Wharf, where a sign in the river wall tells you that you are on The Queen's Walk, inaugurated in 1994. As you approach Blackfriars Bridge, St Paul's Cathedral, and various modern buildings beyond, present one of London's most famous cityscapes. Pass the Doggett's Coat and Badge Inn, pass under the road bridge and continue forward past the Founders Arms to go along Bankside Reach. Next to New Globe Walk can be seen **Shakespeare's Globe Exhibition** and the reconstructed Globe Theatre.

Continue by the river towards Southwark. At the Anchor, Bankside, temporarily leave the river and go under the railway via Clink Street, passing the Clink Prison Museum. Go past the Kathleen and May schooner at Pickfords Wharf, walk to the left of Southwark Cathedral and go past the Mudlark Inn. Do not go under the bridge: instead, turn left up steps leading to London Bridge. Cross the road, with care, and go down the steps in front of the modern Price Waterhouse building. Now continue along the river to Tower Bridge, passing the City Pier, Hay's Galleria and HMS Belfast.

Go up the steps to Tower Bridge and, finally, cross to the north bank. Once over the bridge continue forward on Tower Bridge Approach, then turn left to walk along the northern wall of the Tower of London, following the signs to Tower Hill Underground station from where trains will take you back to Central London (change at Embankment for Waterloo).

POINTS OF INTEREST:
The Museum of the Moving Image – Linked with the National Film Theatre, this Museum provides fascinating displays relating to the world of film and television.
Shakespeare's Globe Exhibition – The exhibition shows how the Globe Theatre has been reconstructed.

REFRESHMENTS:
There are numerous riverside inns and restaurants, some mentioned in the route description, particularly during the second half of the walk. In the earlier section the National Film Theatre Restaurant and Bar is recommended.

Walk 31   DENHAM   4m (6½km)

Maps: OS Sheets Landranger 176; Pathfinder 1158.
A fine walk using village footpaths and a canal towpath.
Start: At 043870, St Mary's Church, Denham.

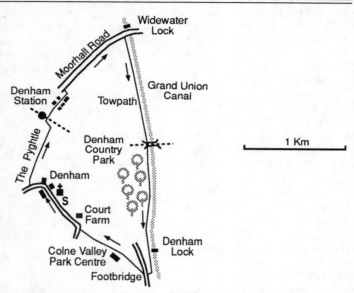

There are actually four 'Denhams' in this area: Denham Green, New Denham, Higher Denham and Denham itself. This walk starts and finishes at the latter, about two miles north-west of Uxbridge. The route skirts Denham Green and includes a section of the Grand Union Canal and parts of Denham Country Park.

From the gate of St Mary's Church, walk along the main street into the village of **Denham**, passing Hills House and several other charming cottages and houses. Where the street curves left, at the green, continue ahead and right down a lane called 'The Pyghtle', passing the gate to Denham Place. Continue along the tarmac footpath, with the golf course to your right. Follow the path around to the left, passing under the railway and Denham Station. Continue along the footpath, passing between the back gardens of Denham Green, to reach a road. Turn left to reach a crossroads. Turn right along Moorhall Road. Shortly, cross the River Colne which is the boundary between Buckinghamshire and Middlesex. The many 'lakes' in this area are the result of gravel excavations.

Continue along Moorhall Road until you pass the Horse and Barge Inn. Shortly after the inn, go down the steps to join the Grand Union Canal towpath. The route goes right, but a detour to the left, under the bridge, is worthwhile to briefly visit Widewater Lock. From the lock go back under the bridge and follow the towpath southwards for about $1\frac{1}{2}$ miles.

After the towpath passes under the railway viaduct, **Denham Country Park** appears on the right. Go under the footbridge and continue along the towpath to reach Denham Lock (the lock-keeper's cottage was built in 1902 and now has a tea garden attached).

About 100 yards after the lock, turn right, leaving the towpath, and cross the footbridge over the Colne. Follow the path to the right and go through a wooden gate. Continue along the path beyond, crossing Misbourne Meadow to reach the corner of a car park. Do not enter the car park: instead, go through the gate, cross the road, and go through another gate (following the arrow waymarkers of the South Bucks Way, a 23 mile route from Wendover to the Grand Union Canal).

Walk past the Colne Valley Park Centre, go through a gate and continue along the edge of a golf course, with the River Misbourne to your left. Shortly, you will reach two gates next to a road bridge: go through these and walk along Village Street to return to Denham Church.

POINTS OF INTEREST:

Denham – Despite its proximity to the M25 and M40 motorways, Denham is a peaceful and picturesque village. It has many attractive houses and cottages, a village green and three inns.

Denham Country Park – This recently-created country park lies between the Grand Union Canal and the River Misbourne, with the River Colne in between. The Colne Valley Park Centre provides information and displays relating to 'the first taste of real countryside on London's western doorstep'.

REFRESHMENTS:
The Swan, Denham.
The Horse and Barge, South Harefield.

Walk 32   BROMPTON AND BELGRAVIA   4m (6¹/₂km)

Maps: OS Sheets Landranger 176; Pathfinder 1175.
Streets, squares and gardens at the heart of London.
Start: At 281787, Sloane Square Underground Station.

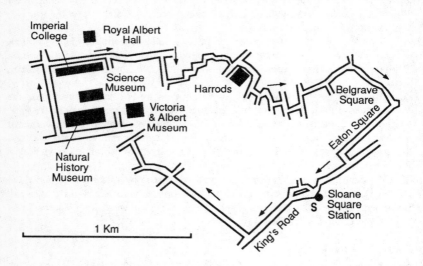

This walk explores the areas of Belgravia and Brompton, including some of the museums of South Kensington. It starts and finishes at Sloane Square.

From the station, go straight across the road and walk along the southern edge of the Square. Continue down King's Road, with its interesting array of shops, for about 400 yards, crossing where convenient to reach Anderson Street, on the right. Walk down this street, and Sloane Avenue beyond, for nearly ¹/₂ mile, then cross at the lights and continue along Pelham Street.

From Pelham Street take the first right, Thurloe Square, and at the end of the Square, turn right and then almost immediately left, through a small garden with a sculpture, 'Twelve Responses to Tragedy' by Angela Conner (almost opposite the Victoria and Albert Museum). Turn left down Cromwell Road and cross at the lights to walk past the main entrance to the **Natural History Museum** (the entrance to the

Science Museum is on Exhibition Road). Turn right, at the end of the Museum grounds, into Queen's Gate and walk past a number of Embassies. Turn right along Prince Consort Road: various departments of Imperial College are to the right and the Royal Albert Hall is on the left. At the end, cross the road and continue down Princes Gardens. Keep ahead as this becomes Ennismore Gardens, and then turn right along Ennismore Mews.

At the end of Ennismore Mews, at the corner where the Ennismore Arms is located, turn left. Go through the gate in the wall on the right into Rutland Street, and then turn left into Montpelier Walk. Most of the houses in this vicinity were built between 1825 and 1850: though originally this was not a highly regarded area, the terraces have great character and there is a certain quiet charm about the locality. Almost immediately turn right into Montpelier Place and, at the end, go left down Montpelier Street. At its end turn right, and at the junction with Trevor Place turn right again. Follow Trevor Place to the left, and then walk along the southern edge of Trevor Square to reach Lancelot Place. Here go right and cross the Brompton Road, with Harrods directly in front of you.

Walk to the left of Harrods, down Hans Cresent, then go right into Basil Street and left into Argentina Place. Follow the one-way street round Hans Place, leaving at Hans Street. At the end of Hans Street, turn right, then left at the crossroads and left again at Cadogan Place. At the end, turn right, cross Lowndes Street and go down West Halkin Street to reach **Belgrave Square**.

Walk forward and right, around the northern corner of the Square. Cross at the eastern corner and go down Belgrave Street. After about 250 yards, turn right into Eaton Square. Walk along here for about $1/_3$ mile, then go left and almost immediately right into Eaton Gate. This leads into Cliveden Place and Sloane Square.

POINTS OF INTEREST:
Natural History Museum – This world-famous Museum attracts over one and a half million visitors a year. The dinosaur skeletons remain the biggest attraction, but there are also modern multi-media displays and in 1995 a Wildlife Garden, illustrating the seven principal habitats of the UK, was opened. The Victorian building, designed by Alfred Waterstone, is regarded as an architectural masterpiece.

Belgrave Square – The Square is in the centre of fashionable Belgravia and has been home to many famous residents. Today the grand terraces tend to house embassies rather than individuals. There are a number of interesting statues in the Square.

REFRESHMENTS:
Ennismore Arms, Ennismore Mews.

Walk 33   KESTON COMMON   4m (6½km)

Maps: OS Sheets Landranger 177; Pathfinder 1192.
Undulating woodland paths and bridleways.
Start: At 419640, Keston Common car park, off the A233.

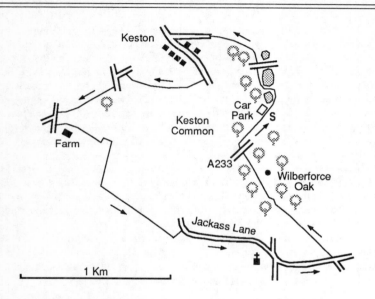

The main part of **Keston Common** is to the west of the car park. Commence the walk by going down the wooden steps near the car park entrance. At the bottom, follow the path to the left, going around the pond. At the end, turn left along a walkway, and then go right down more steps to walk to the left of a second pond. Cross a road and continue past a third pond, going along a bridleway with barriers on either side. Shortly after passing the pond this bridleway meets a crossing path at two wooden barriers: turn left, and then right along a stone path, heading downhill past a bench. Ignore all other paths, following the stone one as it turns to tarmac and passes a school. Continue along a road (Lakes Road) and turn left when you reach the main street (Heathfield Road) in Keston.

   Walk along the main street for about 400 yards, then turn right along an unmade road (Leafy Grove). Where this curves right, continue forward, downhill, along the

68

signposted public footpath. The path crosses two metal stiles and continues to a road. Turn left, and then left again, at the cottage, into Jackass Lane. After 20 yards, turn right along the public footpath signposted to the hamlet of Nash. This path is a steady incline and there are good views back towards Keston.

Soon the path levels out and reaches a lane: turn left, and, after about 40 yards, left again along a footpath marked by the 'Nash Circular Walk' signs. The track passes to the left of Fortune Bank Farm and then goes downhill. At a metal gate follow the waymarked route to the left. This takes you around the end of a field and then heads south. After a further $^1/_4$ mile or so the path turns left to return towards Jackass Lane. The full extent of the woods of Keston Common can now be seen on the skyline to the left.

Turn right at the lane. Ignore a public footpath signposted to Keston Common on the left after about 300 yards and continue along Church Road, going up the hill and past Rectory Road to reach Keston Parish Church. After passing the church, bear half-right along a red tarmac path. Cross next to the roundabout and go along Downe Road. After about $^1/_4$ mile, where this road curves right, just before the junction with Shire Lane, turn left along a footpath which is part of the Farnborough Circular Walk. This path takes you uphill into the woods and over an entrance road to the Holwood Estate. Shortly after you reach the **Wilberforce Oak** and Seat.

Continue forward on the path to reach the main A233 road. Cross, with care, and continue along the footpath almost directly opposite. After about 20 yards, at a crossing of paths, turn right. Now follow the path along the south-eastern edge of Keston Common and back to the car park.

POINTS OF INTEREST:

Keston Common – The Common includes a series of ponds, woods and meadows. It was once part of the Holwood Estate, the former home of William Pitt, the 18th-century Prime Minister. The ancient Caesar's Camp earthworks can be found in the section of Common across the road from the car park.

The Wilberforce Oak – The seat was erected in 1862 to mark the spot, near an oak tree, where William Wilberforce 'after a conversation with Mr Pitt', resolved to bring forward the abolition of the slave trade. The remains of the old oak can still be seen and a new one was planted in 1992. There is a good view down the vale towards Biggin Hill from this famous spot.

REFRESHMENTS:
The Fox Inn, Keston.
There is a picnic site on Keston Common.

Maps: OS Sheets Landranger 177; Pathfinder 1159 and 1175.
Historic streets south of the Thames.
Start: At 312795, Lambeth North Underground Station.

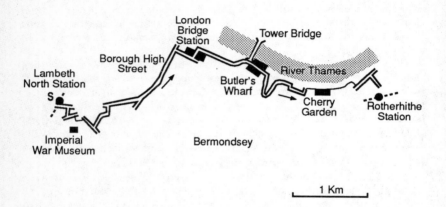

London
Bridge
Station

Tower Bridge

Borough High
Street

Lambeth
North Station

S

River Thames

Butler's
Wharf

Cherry
Garden

Rotherhithe
Station

Imperial
War Museum

Bermondsey

1 Km

From some accounts it would seem that the history of London occurred exclusively on the north bank of the Thames between Westminster and the Tower: this is certainly not the case as this walk south of the river, from Lambeth to Rotherhithe via Southwark and Bermondsey, shows. The second half of the walk includes a fascinating range of docklands architectural styles.

From the station, cross, and walk left along, Westminster Bridge Road for about 300 yards. Turn right, just before the Morley Gallery, into Edward Walk and, at the end, cross to reach the **Imperial War Museum**. Upon leaving the museum, turn right at the battleship guns, go between the bollards and continue to St George's Road. Turn right and cross at the lights to go left down Garden Row. At the end, keep ahead along a minor road and, at the South Bank University building, turn left into Keyworth Street. At the end, turn right along Borough Road. At the main road junction, go left along Borough High Street. Pass Borough Underground Station, with St George-the-

Martyr Church opposite, continuing towards Southwark. Turn right along St Thomas Street, just before London Bridge Station, passing the Old Operating Theatre Museum and parts of Guy's Hospital. Turn left along Stainer Street (actually a tunnel under London Bridge Station) and then go right along Tooley Street. After passing St John's Tavern, divert left through a park area towards the Thames. As you approach the river, turn right to walk under the southern end of Tower Bridge and along Shad Thames, passing the **Butlers Wharf** development and a car park to reach the **Design Museum**.

Go along Maguire Street, away from the river, passing the Clove Building which houses the Bramah Tea and Coffee Museum. At the T-junction, go left and then right on to another part of Shad Thames. Go left past St Saviour's Dock and left again along Mill Street. Follow the road past St Saviour's House, then go right and then left along Chambers Street (if Bermondsey Wall West is closed then use Jacobs Street to reach Chambers Street). Turn left along Bevington Street and into Fountain Green Square. Turn right at the riverside walkway into **Cherry Garden**. Continue past the pier along Bermondsey Wall East, keeping close to the Thames. At the Angel, go along the path to Rotherhithe Village. Go past the 'modernist' Prince's Tower along Elephant Lane to Rotherhithe Street. Go between St Mary's Church and Thames Tunnel Mill and then look out for Brunel's Engine House (used during the construction of the Thames Tunnel) on the right. Turn right at Railway Avenue for Rotherhithe Station from where the Underground can be used to regain the start.

POINTS OF INTEREST:

Imperial War Museum – The building was previously part of the Bethlehem Royal Hospital, or 'Bedlam' lunatic asylum. Since 1920 it has housed displays relating to 20th-century warfare. The conditions of trench warfare and the blitz have been recreated and the Museum has a section of the Berlin Wall.

Butlers Wharf – This stylish warehouse development, together with Tower Bridge Piazza, has a mixture of wine bars, coffee houses and craft shops.

Design Museum – Housed in a converted 'modernist' warehouse, the Museum displays classic items of industrial design.

Cherry Garden – 'Dr Salter's Daydream' consists of three poignant bronze sculptures recreating the vision of Dr Salter (MP for Bermondsey in the 1920s) to improve the quality of life for people living in this part of docklands.

REFRESHMENTS:

The Mayflower Inn, Rotherhithe Street.
The Blueprint Cafe at the Design Museum.

Walk 35   ICKENHAM   4¹/₄m (6³/₄km)

Maps: OS Sheets Landranger 176; Pathfinder 1158.

A circuit of Ickenham, including riverside paths.

Start: At 081860, Ickenham Underground Station (Metropolitan
and Piccadilly Lines, peak hours only).

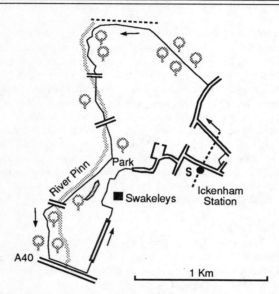

From the station exit, cross the road and turn right. Walk along the road for about 70
yards, and then turn left down the steps. Turn right at the bottom and then left along
Lawrence Drive. After a further 70 yards, turn left, next to No. 72, along an alleyway.
Go straight across the recreation ground to the far right-hand corner and turn left
along Austin's Lane. Follow this lane over the railway and on to reach a main road.

    Cross, with care, and turn right to walk along the High Road (as indicated by the
Hillingdon Trail signs). Just after a shop and before the Soldiers Return Inn, turn left
along a gravel drive leading to a grassy area. Now walk ahead, as indicated by the
waymark post, to reach a bridge. Go past a second post and then walk along another
grassy area. At the metal arrow indicators, do not turn right: instead, keep ahead,
leaving the Hillingdon Trail at this point, to pass to the right of a recreation ground.

The path now continues past the northern corner of the playing field and goes through a gap in the trees to become a broad grass track. Keep close to the railway to reach a stream and a footpath which runs underneath the railway. Do not turn right: instead, bear left on to another green area, keeping close to, and to the left of, the stream (the River Pinn). The route now follows the river for nearly two miles.

Cross the river over the wooden footbridge close to a children's play area and immediately turn left along the western bank. Upon reaching the dual carriageway, cross, with care, and go through a gate to rejoin the river on its left-hand (eastern) side. Go to the right of the tennis courts and then pass between a children's playground and a wooden footbridge to reach a more open area. Cross this, keeping close to the river, to reach a barrier and a road bridge. Cross the road and go right to cross the bridge. After a few more yards, bear left along the cycleway signposted to Uxbridge. This soon bears left and passes to the left of a school. At the end of the school fence, do not go right with the cycleway: instead, keep ahead and slightly left along the footpath going into the trees. Follow this path until it reaches a large wooden fence at the A40. Walk left alongside the fence on a rough track, cross a stream and continue along a rough path for a further 100 yards or so before turning left along a tarmac drive signposted to 'The Grove'. Go past a barrier and keep ahead along the pavement to the left of the grass verges. At the end of The Grove, cross and walk forward along the hedged path just to the left of the entrance to **Swakeleys**.

Follow this path by the fence as it turns left and then right, providing a fine view of the mansion. The path continues beside the river and then reaches a black iron gate. Go through and turn immediately right along the unmade footpath to reach a road. Turn left, and after about 100 yards go right along a road, passing between residential blocks. After this road curves around to the right, turn left along Milton Court. Walk across the corner of the large green area and turn right to reach a main road. Cross, with care, and go left, but soon turn right along Glebe Avenue which leads back to Ickenham Station.

POINTS OF INTEREST:

Swakeleys – This attractive red-brick mansion house was built in the 17th century. The estate was previously much more extensive, but sections of it were sold for residential development in the 1920s. The building is private property.

REFRESHMENTS:
The Fox and Geese, High Road, Ickenham.

Walk 36   **LIMEHOUSE**   4$^1/_4$m (6$^3/_4$km)

Maps: OS Sheets Landranger 177; Pathfinder 1159.
A walk through historic dockside neighbourhoods.
Start: At 362812, Limehouse Docklands Light Railway Station.

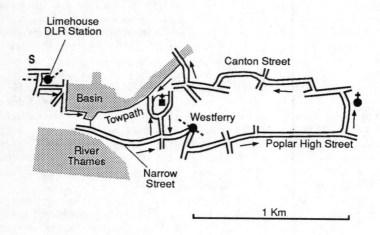

From the Station exit, turn left and then left again at the signpost for Limehouse Basin. At the end of this road, cross and turn right. After about 200 yards, turn left along the walkway to **Limehouse Basin**. Walk along the southern edge of the basin, between a residential block and the yacht marina and, at the end, where there is a plaque on a brick plinth, turn right. Cross the first footbridge, go right and then left along Narrow Street.

Walk past the Grapes and the House They Left Behind inns and, after the Barley Mow Estate, turn left along Three Colt Street. Take the next left, Newell Street, following it around under the railway and past a row of Georgian houses to reach the entrance to **St Anne's Church**, on the right. Walk to the left of, and around, the church, leaving by the gate on to Three Colt Street. Turn right to walk past the Five Bells and Blade Bone inn, and the art-nouveau style Church Institute. Now go under the railway to return to the road junction next to Limehouse Wharf.

At the junction, turn left along Limehouse Causeway. Just before Westferry DLR Station, bear right along the pavement into Westferry. After about 100 yards, cross and go left down Garford Street. Go under the railway and cross the dual carriageway at the lights. Go right, and then half-left down partially pedestrianised Ming Street (the street name is evidence that this was once the Chinese quarter of London), following the signs for Poplar High Street. At the White Horse Inn, keep ahead as Ming Street joins the High Street. Follow this for $^1/_3$ mile until, immediately after crossing the railway, Newby Place appears on the left. Walk along this, passing All Saints Church. At the main road, turn left and, shortly after passing All Saints DLR Station, cross at the lights, but maintain direction, heading westwards along East India Dock Road, passing the Chrisp Street Shopping Centre. After the Tower Hamlets College building, turn right along Sturry Street. At the end, go left along Grundy Street and then keep ahead along Canton Street, to the right of the church, at the crossroads. Follow Canton Street leftwards to meet East India Dock Road once more. Turn right, cross at the lights and turn right into Burdett Road. Shortly after passing the Royal Mail Delivery office, go left down the steps on to the Limehouse Cut towpath. Continue forward on the towpath: it is now $^1/_2$ mile to Limehouse Basin and a further $^1/_3$ mile from the Basin back to the DLR Station.

POINTS OF INTEREST:

Limehouse Basin – The basin is now a yachting marina and the area around it is being redeveloped as a residential area. There are a number of signposted footpaths linking with the Regents Canal, Limehouse Cut and the Thames Path.

St Anne's Church – St Anne's, the Parish Church of Limehouse was designed by Nicholas Hawksmoor, Sir Christopher Wren's assistant. It was consecrated in 1730 and remains a landmark of this part of East London. On the Commercial Road side of the churchyard there is a strange pyramidal structure, also designed by Hawksmoor.

REFRESHMENTS:

The House They Left Behind, Narrow Street.
The Hope and Anchor, Newby Place, Poplar.

Walk 37   ALEXANDRA PALACE $4^1/_4$m ($6^3/_4$km)

Maps: OS Sheets Landranger 176; Pathfinder 1140 and 1159.
Alexandra Palace Park and Queen's Wood.
Start: At 303905, Alexandra Palace Railway Station (trains from Moorgate and Kings Cross).

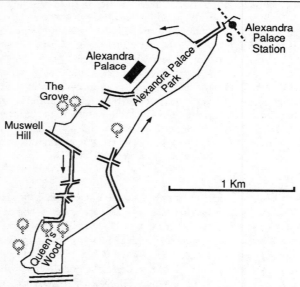

From the station exit, turn left and immediately left again across the footbridge over the railway. At the road, cross and go left. After about 50 yards, pass two bollards and follow a paved path as it ascends into part of Alexandra Palace Park. The path climbs the hill parallel with the road: when it ends near a barrier, turn right along the gravel track, staying on this as it circles the hill. At the crossing of paths next to the animal enclosure, turn left and walk uphill to **Alexandra Palace**. Cross the car park, walk to the left of the TV mast and then go along the front of the building, admiring the views over London. Walk past the Phoenix Bar at the end of the building and go down the steps near the Palm Court Entrance. Cross a road and continue along the path directly opposite into the park. Cross the next road and, from the garden centre entrance, bear right along another path. Pass a barrier to the left of the Grove Car

Park and then go slightly left and ahead along a tree-lined path. Where the path divides, at a green triangle with three trees, keep left. Walk through the footway tunnel, then turn left and left again at the road to walk down Muswell Hill. About 100 yards after the bus stop, cross and go right past the white gate to walk along Cascade Avenue. At the end, go right and then left along The Chine.

At the junction of five roads, cross and make your way up Connaught Gardens. Follow this around to the right to reach an entrance to **Queen's Wood**. Now turn left along the tarmac path signposted to Crouch End and Hornsey. This takes you downhill and across a small stream. Immediately beyond the stream, keep right, uphill, and then take the next path on the left to reach a pond in the middle of the wood. Now go uphill again, along the tarmac path on the far side of the pond. Follow the path to reach Queens Wood Road. Turn left and walk along the road and, after about 150 yards, between the Queenswood Road and Wood Vale signs, turn left along a grass footpath. Keep to the right-hand path closest to the eastern edge of the wood and, as this approaches a wall, bear right along a fenced surfaced path. Cross a road and continue along the path between the tennis courts and playing fields. Cross and go left along Park Road to reach a major set of lights.

Cross Priory Road and walk forward to reach an entrance to Alexandra Palace Park. Walk along the broad park road and, where this goes left, after the car parks, keep forward along a path immediately left of another parking area. Ignore two drives going left, uphill, to Alexandra Palace, continuing along the drive to reach the more open, eastern end of the park. The drive gradually curves left and then straightens out, between a miniature golf course and a nature reserve, to reach a road. Now walk forward to reach the footbridge to Alexandra Palace Station.

POINTS OF INTEREST:

Alexandra Palace – The Palace has a number of claims to fame, perhaps the most notable being its use as the site of the first television transmission in 1936. This momentous event in media history is recorded on a blue plaque. The original building opened in 1873, but was destroyed by fire within 16 days. The later version was also damaged by fire in 1980.

Queen's Wood – This Local Nature Reserve, named after Queen Victoria in 1898, contains 52 acres of woodland and is quieter than neighbouring Highgate Wood.

REFRESHMENTS:

The Phoenix Bar, Alexandra Palace.

Walk 38   TOWER PRECINCTS   4¼m (6¾km)

Maps: OS Sheets Landranger 177; Pathfinder 1159.
A walk along historic East London Streets.
Start: At 336808, Tower Hill Underground Station.

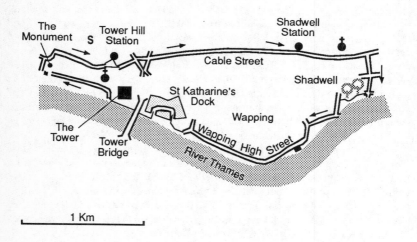

Above the station there is a giant sundial and a Silver Jubilee Walkway plaque identifying the many important buildings in the immediate area. There is also a good view of the Tower of London itself. Upon leaving the station, follow the signs to the Tower Gateway (Docklands Light Railway) Station, passing to the left of a section of the London Wall. Use the subway, and where this emerges at the station entrance, turn immediately right. Now follow the footpath along Shorter Street (between the Hambros building and Sceptre Court). Cross Mansell Street at the lights and continue eastwards along Royal Mint Street. At the crossroads, continue along Cable Street. The elevated railway on the left, and the estates and blocks of flats give this part of the city a particularly urban feel. Follow Cable Street for nearly a mile – this street was the scene of anti-fascist riots in 1936 and aspects of these events are depicted in a mural painted on the side of St George's Town Hall. Walk past Shadwell Station and St Mary's Church, finally turning right at Brodlove Lane. Cross The Highway and enter the King Edward Memorial Park through the gate opposite Brodlove Lane.

The route now returns to the Tower via historic Thames-side paths and streets. Walk beside the river, admiring the views of the Thames and the various Dockland developments. Go through the gate at the western end of the park, turn left at Glamis Road, cross the bridge, and then turn left, following the Riverside Walkway path for a short distance. This ends by the Prospect of Whitby Inn, where you should turn left. Continue along Wapping Wall, passing Metropolitan Wharf, Jubilee Wharf and New Crane Wharf. Turn left at Garnet Street to see more evidence of the 'gentrification' of this part of Docklands. Go past Wapping Station and continue along Wapping High Street, passing a small public park at Wapping New Stairs. Now follow the High Street round as it becomes St Katharines Way. At the end, walk to the right of the white building to enter **St Katharine's Dock**.

Walk past the Dickens Inn and the shops, cross the footbridge and walk to the front of the Tower Hotel. At this point the 'Girl With a Dolphin Statue' (Wynne, 1973) can be seen and there is a much-photographed perspective of Tower Bridge. Continue under the northern end of the bridge and go along the cobbled Tower precincts. Traitors' Gate can be seen to the right. Follow the precinct rightwards, passing the Tower entrance and going through a gate. Turn immediately left into Lower Thames Street, passing the Custom House. Just before reaching London Bridge, go up the steps and over the footbridge. Turn left at the end of the bridge to reach Fish Street Hill and then right to visit **The Monument**. From here, turn left up Pudding Lane and then right into Eastcheap. Continue ahead as this becomes Great Tower Street, then cross and bear left opposite the Church of All Hallows by the Tower. Now go through Trinity Square Gardens to return to Tower Hill Station.

POINTS OF INTEREST:

St Katharine's Dock – Redeveloped in the 1970s, the Dock area is worth further exploration. It includes a yachting marina, historic ships, warehouses, the Tower Hotel, the 18th-century Dickens Inn and a new shopping complex.

The Monument – Designed by Wren, the Monument is 202 feet high and has 311 steps. It commemorates the Great Fire of London of 1666 which started in nearby Pudding Lane.

REFRESHMENTS:

The Prospect of Whitby, allegedly a haunted pub, Wapping Wall.
The Dickens, St Katharine's Dock.

Walk 39   **HORTON COUNTRY PARK** $4\frac{1}{4}$m ($6\frac{3}{4}$km)
Maps: OS Sheets Landranger 176; Pathfinder 1190.
Easy Country Park and footpath walking.
Start: At 179633, Chessington (South) Railway Station.

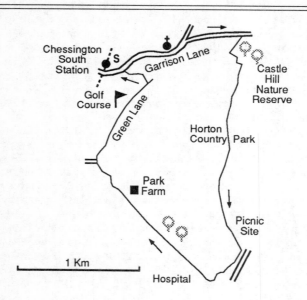

From the station exit, turn left and walk up Garrison Lane for $\frac{1}{4}$ mile to reach
Chessington Parish Church. Follow the pavement around, passing the 12th-century
church and continuing along Church Lane. After about 100 yards, cross and bear
half-right down Stokesby Road (opposite St Mary's Hall). This road soon emerges at
a green oval traffic island with a number of shops on either side: cross the green
using the paved section and go left, and then right down Filby Road. Shortly, turn
right along the signposted Hogsmill Walk. This leads into **Castle Hill** Nature Reserve
and Horton Country Park.

Keep on the main stone path as it winds it way through the Reserve. Shortly
after passing between wooden barriers the path forms a T-junction with a bigger track:
turn right. After about $\frac{1}{2}$ mile the track forks either side of a wooden bench: take the
left-hand fork which is signposted as part of the 'Chessington Countryside Walk'.

Ignore footpaths going off to the left and the right, continuing along the main, waymarked walk/horseride. Pass to the right of a polo field and go through a Horton Country Park gate. Where the drive forms a T-junction with another track, keep ahead through a further wooden gate and walk down a tree-lined, fenced footpath (again indicated as the Chessington Countryside Walk). The path passes a picnic site, to the left, and then bears right to run parallel with a road. After about 100 yards, bear half-left off the main track along a smaller path into the trees. This path takes the walker over a small tarmac drive, across two fields and into a small wooded section. At a gate near a length of silver piping, turn right.

Follow this new path for about a mile. Beyond the green wire fence on the left are the buildings of West Park Hospital. The footpath can be quite narrow and overgrown here, but it soon reaches a stile and an open field. Go over the stile and maintain direction across the field, keeping the small wire fence to your left. Some of the rides at **Chessington World of Adventures** can be glimpsed on the hill ahead and to the left. Cross two more stiles close to Park Farm, then go over the concrete drive and another stile to reach a footpath signposted to Chessington. Cross the field, go over a stile and then bear left along a tarmac lane. Where this bends sharply left, keep ahead along the footpath to Chessington. Continue along the lane for $\frac{1}{2}$ mile, a golf course shortly appearing on the left and houses soon appearing on the right. Where the lane begins to go uphill more steeply, opposite the entrance to Green Lane Nurseries, turn left along the footpath to Garrison Lane. This skirts the 17th green and then goes up a steep grassy bank. At the top of the bank, walk left and admire the view. At the wooden post turn right along a footpath going into the undergrowth and then downhill to Garrison Lane. Turn left at the bottom to return to the station.

POINTS OF INTEREST:
Castle Hill – This local Nature Reserve was once part of a deer park and contains the site of a medieval hunting lodge. Roe deer still occasionally visit these woodlands.
Chessington World of Adventures – This popular tourist attraction is only a few minutes walk from Chessington (South) Station if you want to make a day of it.

REFRESHMENTS:
None on the route, but there is a picnic site in Horton Country Park.

Walk 40   CHASE NATURE RESERVE $4^1/_2$m ($7^1/_4$km)

Maps: OS Sheets Landranger 177; Pathfinder 1160.
A circular exploration of a Nature Reserve.
Start: At 526857, Elm Park Underground Station.

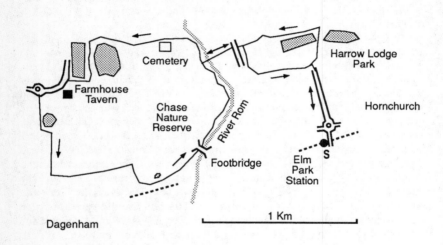

From the station exit turn left and, at the roundabout, continue ahead along Elm Parade and St Nicholas Avenue. At the end, go past the barrier to enter Harrow Lodge Park. Follow the tarmac path and cross the footbridges between the two lakes. After the second bridge, leave the path and take to the grass along the northern edge of the left-hand lake, with railings and then a number of willow trees to your left. At the end of the lake, bear right along a path towards a number of houses and garages. As you reach these, do not leave the park: instead, turn left along a footpath between the trees, then go forward on the grass to reach a road at the western edge of the park.

Cross Rainham Road and go right for a short distance before turning left along a drive signposted as 'Bridleway 180'. This leads into the **Chase Nature Reserve**. Shortly after crossing the River Rom, go right through a gap in the wooden fence and follow the path beside the river. Take the first prominent path on the left – after about $^1/_4$ mile – heading away from the river. As the path approaches the railings, bear right,

82

walk alongside the railings and past the cemetery. At the far corner of the cemetery, fork right off the bank and follow the prominent grass track, passing to the right of the lake which can be seen ahead. Just before reaching a road, go left through a gap in the fence. Walk to the lake's edge, go right over a bank and then left along a well-defined path on the bank between the two lakes. As you approach a tarmac drive, bear right along a smaller footpath around the southern end of the right-hand lake. After 120 yards, fork left to leave the Reserve temporarily. At the road, turn left and then follow the road rightwards past the Farmhouse Tavern. Walk to the mini-roundabout and then go left along the public footpath towards Rainham Road South. Follow the gravel track to the right of a lake, go left along the top edge of the lake and then right along another gravel track, ignoring a route to the left. Now keep ahead, between the small green barriers, to go along a hedged footpath, with a sports ground on the left and a car park on the right. At the end, go left along the tarmac footpath signposted to Hornchurch.

Where the tarmac turns to grass, keep ahead to reach a gate into the Nature Reserve. Go through and follow the path closest to the green fence. At the corner, turn right and walk alongside the green fence to reach a stile by the railway. Do not cross the stile: instead, turn left and walk beside the railway fence. There are a variety of paths here, none of them particularly well-defined. In general keep close to the southern boundary of the Reserve until the river appears on your right. Do not cross the river at the footbridge: instead, walk beside it on the paths close to its left bank. After about $\frac{1}{2}$ mile, as you approach the next bridge, look for a stile in the fence on the left. Climb this and then go right along the bridleway used in the early stages of the walk. Cross Rainham Road and walk along the western edge of Harrow Lodge Park, staying close to the road to join a tarmac path which goes around the tennis courts. Where this path leads to an exit, continue forward on the grass, going along the southern edge of the park. The third exit on the right now leads to St Nicholas Avenue and the start.

POINTS OF INTEREST:
Chase Nature Reserve – Much of the swathe of green between Hornchurch and Dagenham is now a London Wildlife Trust Nature Reserve. The walk described here is an exploratory circuit of the various habitats, including grassland, meadows, lakes and riverside. The River Rom forms a natural boundary between the boroughs of Havering and Barking and Dagenham.

REFRESHMENTS:
The Farmhouse Tavern, Dagenham Road.

Walk 41   BENTLEY PRIORY CIRCUIT $4\frac{1}{2}$m ($7\frac{1}{4}$km)

Maps: OS Sheets Landranger 176; Pathfinder 1139.

A woodland and common circular walk.

Start: At 160936, Stanmore Common car park, Warren Lane (off the A4140).

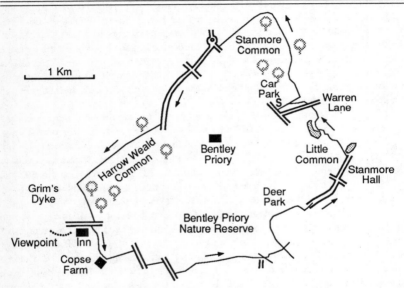

Leave the car park by following the footpath immediately to the right of the Bentley Priory Circular Walk information board. After about 200 yards the path reaches a tarmac drive: turn left just before the gate on to the horseride marked by white posts. Stay on this track as it loops around the edges of Stanmore Common to emerge at a roundabout. From Heathbourne Road, cross and go left along Magpie Hall Road. At the lights, cross and continue along Common Road. After a further $\frac{1}{4}$ mile, turn right along a footpath signposted to Old Redding. Follow this well-defined path close to the northern (right-hand) edge of **Harrow Weald Common**. Soon the path curves left and reaches a crossing of paths: keep ahead, as indicated by the yellow arrow. The path now runs beside a ditch and turns left at a cottage called 'The Bothy'. A few yards further on, keep left and then right, still on the route of the Circular Walk, waymarked by yellow arrows. At the gate, cross the road and turn right. Walk along the road past The Case is Altered Inn to reach a car park and picnic area. This is a fine local viewpoint: Harrow-on-the-Hill can be seen in the middle distance.

After visiting the viewpoint, walk back along the road and, beyond the inn, turn right along the drive to a riding school. Walk past Copse Farm and go left along the drive signposted to Brookshill. At the end, turn right, walk along the road for just over 100 yards and then cross and go left along a downhill path at another Circular Walk sign. This path reaches another road: cross and turn right. Shortly, turn left at another Circular Walk sign to go along the drive to Lower Priory Farm. Walk to the right of the farm on a footpath, accompanied by a ditch, which soon reaches an entrance to **Bentley Priory Nature Reserve** on the left.

Enter the reserve and walk to the right of (and behind) the information board to reach a small gap in a wooden barrier fence. Go along a path over a stream to reach a surfaced footpath. Turn left. Go through a wooden gate and, after 20 yards, turn right along a raised path next to the deer enclosure fence. Walk uphill on the grass beside the fence. As you approach the end of the enclosure the path bears right and then left to reach a wooden kissing gate: go through the gate and along the residential lane (Aylmer Drive) beyond. Cross the main road, with care, and continue along Wood Lane. Walk past Stanmore Hall and then go left along the footpath between Fairview Cottage and the pond. Walk past the corrugated iron building and then bear left across the grass to converge with an unmade road. Pass between the metal barriers and onto the sports field. Turn left and, at the corner of the field, go right as indicated by the yellow arrows. Follow the path around the edge of the lake and, at the end, keep left between this lake and a pond to pass Stanmore Cricket Club. Cross Warren Lane to join a smaller path on to Stanmore Common. Where this path forks, bear left and then keep forward across a tarmac drive to return to the car park.

POINTS OF INTEREST:

Harrow Weald Common – The Common is part of the ancient forest of Middlesex. The wilderness once covered an area of nearly 1,500 acres but is now down to about 45 acres. In the 18th century the Common was a haunt of highwaymen. The Grim's Dyke earthwork runs along the Common's northern edge.

Bentley Priory Nature Reserve – The Reserve comprises sections of woodland, scrub and grassland along with a lake and a number of ponds. Tawny Owls and Kestrels breed in the woods.

REFRESHMENTS:

The Case is Altered Inn, Old Redding.

85

Walk 42   BUSHY PARK   4¹/₂m (7¹/₄km)

Maps: OS Sheets Landranger 176; Pathfinder 1174 and 1190.

A circular walk around the second largest Royal Park.

Start: At 160694, the Diana Fountain car park, at the centre of Bushy Park.

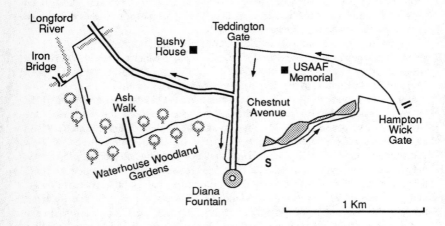

From the far end of the car park, walk along the nearest edge of the Model Boating Pool. Continue alongside Heron Pond, following the path around the end of the pond. Now, just before the low brick footbridge, turn right to walk alongside the waterway leading to Leg-of-Mutton Pond. Follow the path around the eastern end of the pond to reach a tarmac footpath. Turn right along this, heading for Hampton Wick Gate. Do not go through the Gate: instead, turn sharp left to follow the broad path running close to the wall of the park. Follow this path for about ¹/₂ mile to reach a fenced plaque in the grass, about 200 yards to the left: this is the **USAAF Memorial.** From the memorial return to the perimeter path and continue to reach the Teddington Gate and Chestnut Avenue, the public road traversing the park. Do not cross the road: instead, turn left and walk alongside it. Deer are frequently seen in this section of the park.

After about 500 yards there is a turning to the right, signposted to three Lodges and Bartons Cottage. Cross Chestnut Avenue and walk alongside the road. Pass a car park and continue ahead along Upper Lodge Road to reach a small, low footbridge with white posts and railings. Cross the bridge and turn immediately left to walk alongside a small waterway: there is a grass path here but it is not very well defined. Walk towards the grey fence, then turn left and walk beside the fence until you reach a wooden gate and an information board. From here a short detour is worthwhile: go right, through the gate, and follow the path beyond for about 200 yards to view the tranquil Longford River and the Iron Bridge. From the bridge retrace your steps back to the wooden gate. Do not go through the gate: instead, turn right just before it at another gate, to enter **Waterhouse Woodland Gardens**. Walk forward along the broad grass pathway between the trees and, after passing the buildings of River Lodge and the remains of a large tree trunk, fork left on to a path going between silver birch trees. Cross a green wooden footbridge and follow the path as it curves right, left and right again, to reach a gate by a Royal Parks Constabulary telephone box.

Go across Ash Walk to the next wooden gate to enter the eastern plantation. Keep to the main path through the centre of the plantation, shortly passing to the right of Triss's Pond. Ignore the path to the left, continuing ahead on 'Taxodium Walk' (named after the nearby Water Cypress trees). Shortly you will reach Crocodile Bridge, named after an oak tree on the other side of the waterway, felled in the 1987 hurricane, which does bear an uncanny resemblance to a crocodile. Leave the gardens by the gate next to Crocodile Bridge and head straight across the grass to reach a road. Do not cross the road: instead, turn right and walk under the chestnut trees to the Diana Fountain. The car park can now be seen across the road to the left.

POINTS OF INTEREST:
USAAF Memorial – This memorial commemorates the fact that Bushy Park was used as an American airbase during the Second World War. Chestnut Avenue was an airstrip and there were numerous buildings for the airforce personnel.

Waterhouse Woodland Gardens – These gardens, with their ponds, waterfalls and exotic trees, provide a scenic finale to the walk and are worth exploring in detail.

REFRESHMENTS;
None on the route, but there is a picnic area next to the Diana Fountain car park.

Walk 43   FAIRLOP WATERS $4\frac{1}{2}$m ($7\frac{1}{4}$km)

Maps: OS Sheets Landranger 177; Pathfinder 1141.
A fine Country Park and lakeside walk.
Start: At 449907, Fairlop Underground Station.

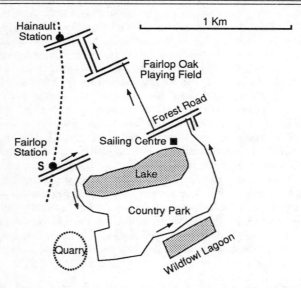

The countryside featured in this walk presents a good illustration of how land can be reclaimed from industrial use for recreational purposes. Fairlop Waters provides a pleasant area for walkers, bird-watchers and watersports enthusiasts. The route starts at Fairlop Underground Station and finishes at Hainault Station, both of which are on the Central line.

    Leave Fairlop Station and turn left along Forest Road, passing under the railway bridge. After about 400 yards, cross over to enter **Fairlop Waters Country Park,** on the right. Walk between the lake and the restaurant building, then continue along the gravel track as it curves round the western end of the lake, with part of a golf course on your right.

Shortly, bear right along a grass path, going slightly uphill away from the lake. After about 100 yards, turn right once more, this time along another grass path going gently downhill through scrubland. This path joins a sandy/gravel track: continue along this track to reach a fork. Take the left branch, following it along a straight section, with a hedgerow and an excavation site to your right.

Where the gravel track curves left, continue ahead along a broad grass path. At the corner, turn left and follow the footpath along the southern edge of the Country Park, with a stream on your right. Keep to this grass footpath until it joins a gravel track and emerges at a grass clearing with a building ahead. Now turn right and walk towards the wooden fence. Go through the gap in the fence to visit the 'Birdwatching and Feeding Area' next to the Wildfowl Lagoon. It is not possible to walk right around the Lagoon, so retrace your steps back to the fence and walk along its northern edge, ignoring a tarmac path going left to the car park.

At the end of the lake you will reach the corner of a fence: turn left, and then right along the entrance road to the Fairlop Sailing Centre. Follow this road to leave the Country Park, then turn left and walk along Forest Road. After about 300 yards, go right into the car park for Fairlop Oak Playing Field. Walk through the car park and across the corner of the playing field to reach a tarmac footpath on its left-hand side. Follow this path to the end of the playing fields, then turn left along a track passing between a hedge and a number of garages. Shortly, turn right and continue to a road. Walk down the road (Lancelot Road) and at the end turn left to reach Hainault Station.

POINTS OF INTEREST:

Fairlop Waters Country Park – During the Second World War Fairlop Waters was an airfield. After the war it was used as a refuse and gravel excavation site. The area has now been reclaimed and the Country Park and the golf course together provide about 400 acres of recreational land.

REFRESHMENTS:

Daltons American Diner and Bar, Fairlop Country Park.

Walk 44   OSTERLEY PARK   4$\frac{1}{2}$m (7$\frac{1}{4}$km)

Maps: OS Sheets Landranger 176; Pathfinder 1174.
A varied walk through fields and along parkland footpaths.
Start: At 145771, Osterley Underground Station.

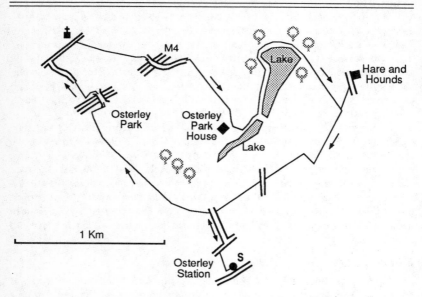

From the station exit (on the Great West Road), turn right and almost immediately right again along a paved path, going over the railway. Continue down the steps and along the fenced alleyway. At the road (Bassett Gardens) turn right, then, after about 100 yards, go left. At the end, cross over and go through the gap in the wall. Turn left on to a track along the edge of the field. Shortly, where the track bears left at the start of a hedgerow, keep ahead, walking to the right of the hedgerow. The fenced plantation over to the right is part of Osterley Park.

After a while the path switches to the other side of the hedgerow and cuts through a wooded area to reach the footbridge over the M4. Shortly after crossing the motorway the path ends at a gate on to a lane. Turn left along the lane, following it around to the right to reach its junction with Tentelow Lane at **Norwood Green**.

Turn right along the road to reach the Parish Church and the Plough Inn. Immediately after the inn, turn right along the footpath signposted to St Mary's Avenue. Cross the road and continue along the footpath between fences and then across a field. This is one of several points on the route where you can expect to see aircraft about to land at Heathrow Airport.

Go up steps to join Osterley Lane, which crosses the motorway once more. Keep forward along the lane, passing the walled Osterley Park Farm, and then bear right along the drive between two lodges to enter the main part of Osterley Park. When you reach the corner of the stable block, turn right and go through a black gate to reach the front of **Osterley Park House**. From the house, continue along the main drive beside the lake. This is 'Garden Lake' with its distinctive Chinese Pavilion. Do not walk right around the end of the lake: instead, bear left, go through another black gate and walk to the left of a second, larger lake. Follow the path beside this lake, with North-East Meadow to your left. Keep close to the water, bearing left and then right into a wooded area. At the far, northern, end of the lake (near the motorway) there is a kissing gate made of wooden stakes. Go through this, and turn right along the bridleway (Osterley Lane).

Follow the lane towards Wyke Green, soon reaching a gateway between South Lodge and Wyke Green Lodge. Turn left here if refreshments are needed: it is a short detour to the Hare and Hounds. Turn right after the Lodge and walk along the edge of the green to continue the walk. This path passes behind some back gardens and turns right, and then left, before reaching Osterley Park's tree-lined main drive. Go straight across the drive and continue to reach the gap in the wall used earlier. Now cross the road and retrace your outward route back to Osterley Station.

POINTS OF INTEREST:

Norwood Green – With its green, church and inns, Norwood Green manages to maintain its village charm despite the proximity of the M4 motorway. Until 1963 the green was the scene of an annual cricket match between two of the village inns.

Osterley Park House – The House dates from the 16th century, with additions by William Chambers and Robert Adam. It is now in the care of the National Trust and the spectacular interior attracts many visitors.

REFRESHMENTS:

The Hare and Hounds, Wyke Green.
There is a tea room in the Osterley House Stable Block.

Walk 45   BEDFORDS PARK   4½m (7¼km)

Maps: OS Sheets Landranger 177; Pathfinder 1141.

A Country Park and Havering village.

Start: At 520924, the car park at Bedfords Park, Havering-atte-Bower.

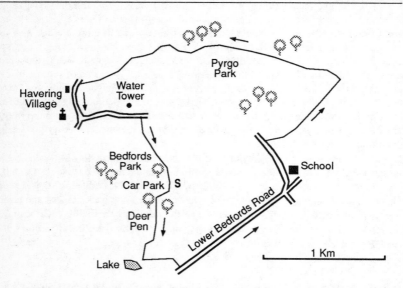

Use the main car park in the centre of **Bedfords Park**, the one furthest away from the Havering Road. Leave the car park by the main path heading southwards, signposted to the deer park and cafe. Soon the cafe can be seen to the left. Continue along the left-hand side of the fenced deer pen and, after about 400 yards, bear right over a small wooden bridge. Follow the path beyond, keeping close to the wire fence of the deer pen. After a further 200 yards or so, as you pass the south end of the pen, bear half-left along another grass path waymarked as part of a circular walk. This path leads into an open field and then heads down to Bedfords Lake. About 20 yards from the lake, go left over a wooden plank and uphill along the prominent grass path beyond. Keep ahead as this path joins a track. At the T-junction with another track, turn left and, after about 40 yards, turn right along a smaller footpath between two trees. Follow this grass path as it goes gently uphill and then heads towards the corner of a meadow. At the corner, turn right to reach a road. Cross and walk left along Lower Bedfords Road for about $^1/_3$ mile.

As you approach a school, cross the dual carriageway, with care, and go left along Broxhill Road. Shortly after the road begins to go downhill, turn right over a stile on to a footpath signposted to Cummings Hall Lane. Cross a stile and walk along the edge of a field to reach a small wooden bridge. Cross this and another stile nearby and follow the narrow fenced path beyond. Cross six more stiles and then keep ahead along a narrow, sometimes overgrown, section of path to reach a farm drive near a caravan park. Turn left and walk along the drive, with the farm to your left. Go over a stile next to a double gate and straight across the field beyond to reach another stile. Cross this and turn right to walk along the field edge, with a small wood to your right.

At the end of the wood, turn left along the footpath signposted to Havering Village. Havering's distinctive water tower can be seen ahead and there are good views in all directions. The path goes left through a black metal kissing gate to enter Pyrgo Park: follow the track around the top edge of the field and, at the next signpost, go left over a stile. Walk beside the southern edge of the wood, turning right at the first corner of the wood and left at the next corner, as indicated by the footpath signposts. The path now takes you to the right of the end of a plantation and then across a field. Go over a wooden footbridge and head half-right across another field to reach its far right-hand corner, using the yellow arrow-marked posts for guidance. From the corner, bear slightly right along the edge of another field, with a hedgerow to your left. At the road, near the Willows Inn, turn left and walk past Rose Cottage and the village green. Go left along Broxhill Road and, shortly after passing a cricket ground, enter Bedfords Park on the right.

POINTS OF INTEREST:
Bedfords Park – This pleasant Country Park includes woods, meadows, a lake, playing fields, a deer pen and an extensive nature trail. Since much of the park is on hills there are good views south and towards London.

REFRESHMENTS:
The Willows Inn, North Road, Havering-atte-Bower.
There is also a cafe in Bedfords Park.

Walk 46   BLACKHEATH COMMON   4½m (7¼km)

Maps: OS Sheets Landranger 177; Pathfinder 1175 and 1176.
A circuit of Blackheath Common.
Start: At 396760, Blackheath Rail Station.

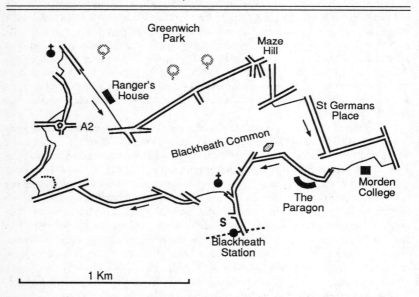

Though not as famous as adjoining Greenwich Park, Blackheath Common has a fascinating history and several interesting buildings on its fringes.

From the Station turn left along Tranquil Vale. Where the road forks, use the pedestrian crossing to keep right into Montpelier Vale. As you go up the hill bear left to reach All Saints Church, a landmark on the southern edge of **Blackheath Common**. Walk across a section of the Common on the path from the south-west corner of the church, ignoring two paths going right to reach a mini-roundabout. Cross and follow Hare and Billet Lane ahead and then right. After passing the Hare and Billet Ale House, fork left along Eliot Place. Follow the road as it dips into a residential area and emerges to the left of another stretch of Common. At the main junction, go left along Mounts Pond Road and down Eliot Hill. After passing The Knoll, turn right and walk on the grass beside a minor road. Towards the end of this, bear right, staying on the grass beside Wat Tyler Road. Opposite the Territorial Army Centre, fork left slightly, across the road, and go along Dartmouth Terrace. The full extent of the Common can be seen to the right.

At the end of the terrace, follow the road around to the left for a short distance and then cross the A2 at the pedestrian crossing. Walk half-right on a path across the grass and then go left down Hyde Vale. About 30 yards before the Diamond Terrace street sign, cross and go right up a set of steps. Half-way up the hill, turn left along a gravel path. Keep left after St Ursula's School to reach Our Ladye Star of the Sea Church. There, cross and bear right up Croom Hills. Follow the sign to the Ranger's House and walk along tree-lined Chesterfield Walk. At the road, turn left into Charlton Way. Cross and walk along the northern edge of the Common, with the wall to Greenwich Park on your left. Cross Duke Humphrey Road at the mini-roundabout next to Blackheath Gate and maintain direction along the edge of the Common. Cross two more roads at the junction with Maze Hill and then bear half-right along a concrete path. On reaching a road (Vanburgh Terrace), turn right. At the end, cross Shooter's Hill Road and immediately turn left to walk on the grass parallel with the road. After about 250 yards, as you approach the lights, turn right to cross another road and go along St Germans Place on the eastern fringe of the Common. At the roundabout, go left along Kidbrooke Gardens, and at the mini-roundabout turn right along Kidbrooke Grove. About 200 yards down this road, turn right along a footpath, following it around the grounds of **Morden College**. Go through the green metal gate at the end and keep ahead. Cross the road and go right along the pavement, with a crescent called 'The Paragon' to your left. Continue past Cator Manor and a pond to reach a junction with the main road. Turn left beyond the Princess of Wales Inn and walk along Montpelier Vale back to Blackheath Village and Station.

POINTS OF INTEREST:
Blackheath Common – The Common has a long history, dating back to at least Roman times. It has been used for mass gatherings, royal pageantry and military rallies. In recent years it has been used as the mass start area for the London Marathon. The Common is bordered on three sides by terraces of fine houses, including 'The Paragon', a crescent built in the early 19th century.
Morden College – Built in 1695 for Sir John Morden, a shipping merchant, the college today contains residences for the elderly.

REFRESHMENTS:
The Hare and Billet Ale House, Hare and Billet Road.
The Princess of Wales, Prince of Wales Road.

Walk 47　　　　TRENT PARK　　　　4½m (7¼km)

Maps: OS Sheets Landranger 176; Pathfinder 1140.

A walk through a woodland Country Park.

Start: At 281964, Cockfosters Underground Station,
　　　or at 281969, the car park at Trent Country Park.

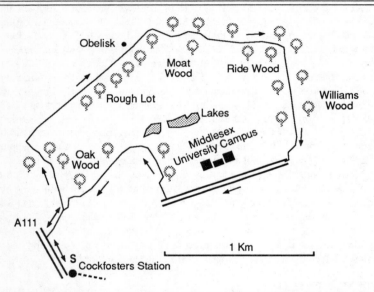

From the station exit, turn right and walk along Cockfosters Road, passing a garage
and the cemetery gates to reach the main entrance to **Trent Country Park**. Walk along
the main entrance road and, near the small obelisk, bear left along a track into the
large grass and gravel car parking area (the alternative start). Walk through this car
park and across the next field to its top left-hand corner. There, turn left (with the
water tower prominent ahead) and, after about 20 yards, turn right along a footpath
into the woods, as indicated by a nature trail marker post.

　　　The path winds through the wood and goes close to the road on the western edge
of the park before curving right. The path is well-defined here, passing between two
open fields and then entering a wooded area called 'Rough Lot'. Ignore paths to the
right and continue forward until you reach another, much taller, obelisk. At this obelisk

do not turn right: instead, continue ahead along a track. After about 100 yards this track bears right (as indicated by another marker post), to pass through Moat Wood: continue to a fork. Take the left branch, then keep ahead where there is a major crossing of paths near a toilet block. Continue through Ride Wood crossing two more tracks and a bridleway.

Soon, near the north-eastern corner of the park, the track curves right and heads downhill into Williams Wood. Go through double wooden gates and cross a stream. Continue forward at the next double gate, following the track to pass a gate and some houses. The straight concrete drive now passes a car park and buildings which are part of the Middlesex University complex.

Cross the road (signposted to the campus) and continue ahead for about 150 yards to reach a gate. Just before the gate, turn right along a footpath which returns to the recreational part of the park passing a number of animal pens on the right. Cross a drive and bear half-right along a gravel track signposted to 'The Lakes'. At the information board, turn right if you wish to visit the lakes. The walk turns left, however, going along the path beside the hedgerow. When this path reaches Oak Wood, do not go into the wood: instead, bear half-left along the grass track by the south-eastern edge of the wood. This track takes you to a tarmac drive: turn right to return to the car park and the entrance road. Now reverse the outward route to return to the station.

POINTS OF INTEREST:
Trent Country Park – Part of the area known as 'Enfield Chase', this Country Park provides over 600 acres of recreational land. The southern part of the Park contains the Middlesex University campus, but the woods, lakes and fields provide much interest for walkers and wildlife enthusiasts.

REFRESHMENTS:
There is a cafeteria and several picnic areas in Trent Country Park.

Walk 48   SYON PARK   4½m (7¼km)

Maps: OS Sheets Landranger 176; Pathfinder 1174 and 1175.

On streets, a towpath and through parkland.

Start: At 204772, Chiswick Railway Station.

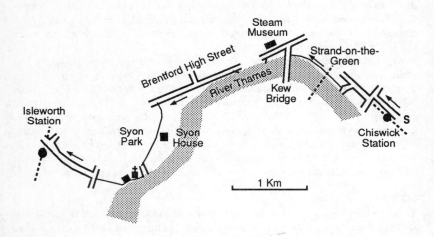

The route roughly follows the north side of the Thames from Chiswick to Isleworth, via Strand-on-the-Green, Kew Bridge, Brentford and Syon Park, finishing at Isleworth Railway Station from where there are frequent trains back to Chiswick.

From the Chiswick Station forecourt, turn left to walk along Burlington Lane. After about 300 yards, go up the steps on the left and cross the railway bridge. Turn right at the next street, Grove Park Gardens, continuing forward at the crossroads to go along the partially-pedestrianised Riverview Grove. Turn left into Riverview Road and, at the end, cross over and bear right along the Thames Path. The delightful Strand-on-the-Green offers the thirsty walker a choice of three riverside inns.

Continue along the Thames Path as it passes well-kept houses and gardens and eventually reaches Kew Bridge. Cross the approach road at the lights and head down

Kew Bridge Road (signposted 'Syon House $2\frac{1}{4}$') passing the **Kew Bridge Steam Museum**. Shortly, pass Victoria Steps Quay and divert left into Watermans Park. The church on the right is a Music Museum.

Now walk past the moored boats and bear right to leave Watermans Park, passing the Watermans Arts Centre. Continue along Brentford High Street for about a mile, then, shortly after going over a bridge across the Grand Union Canal, pass the George and Dragon Inn and a small parade of shops. Turn left down the entrance road to Syon Park (signposted as the Pedestrian Entrance to the Park). Walk past the Brent Lea Recreation Ground on a walled, tarmac drive, going past a number of houses and the entrances to Syon Park Gardens and the Butterfly House to reach **Syon House** and the main park.

After visiting the house, continue westwards through the park on the grass beside the main driveway. As you leave the park, turn left and walk beside the Thames once more, passing All Saints, the Parish Church of Isleworth and the London Apprentice Tavern. Continue along Church Street for a further 200 yards, passing modern residential developments, and then turn right down Mill Plat. You now pass a number of almshouses and Silverhall Nature Park. Cross the Twickenam Road, go right for a short distance and then left along Linkfield Road. At the end, turn left to reach Isleworth Station.

POINTS OF INTEREST:
Kew Bridge Steam Museum – The Steam Museum, one of London's lesser-known museums, is housed within the former Grand Junction Water Pumping Station. It contains, amongst other things, the world's largest beam engine and a narrow-gauge steam railway.
Syon House – Robert Adam's house has a splendid 18th-century interior. The gardens and park were landscaped by Capability Brown. The nearby London Butterfly House contains hundreds of species of butterflies and moths and is a popular tourist attraction. The park has the misfortune to be directly under the flight path to Heathrow Airport!

REFRESHMENTS:
The City Barge, Strand-on-the-Green.
The London Apprentice, Isleworth.

Walk 49   SELSDON WOOD   4¹/₂m (7¹/₄km)

Maps: OS Sheets Landranger 187 or 177; Pathfinder 1191.
A figure of eight walk around Selsdon and neighbouring woods.
Start: At 357616, the car park at Selsdon Wood Nature Reserve, off the Selsdon to Farleigh Road.

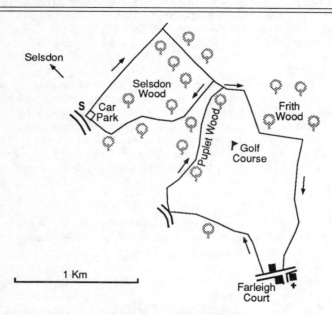

Walk to the far end of the grass section of the car park and keep ahead along the grass track, going downhill. The track takes you between trees and into a clearing: keep to the left side of the field, maintaining direction along the north-western edge of **Selsdon Wood**. The prominent path now passes through more trees, goes to the left of another clearing and enters the main part of the wood, with a green railing fence on the left. Shortly after the railings give way to a wire fence, turn right along a prominent track which rises fairly steeply into the wood.

    After about 150 yards, the track reaches a crossing of paths next to a wooden bench. Continue ahead here and at the next two path crossings, following the track as it goes downhill and ignoring a major path on the right, to reach a metal gate at the north-eastern corner of the wood. Go through the gate and continue ahead, crossing another path. Stay on the path as it goes down and then up (with a recently-constructed golf course to your right) to reach the edge of Frith Wood. There, follow the bridleway on the right, with the wood on your immediate left and the golf course and a view of Selsdon Wood to the right.

The bridleway turns left to skirt the southern edge of Frith Wood and then meets another, crossing, bridleway: turn right along this new bridleway, following it for approximtely $^2/_3$ mile to reach a road opposite Farleigh Court, with St Mary's Church visible some way ahead. Turn right and walk along the road for about 150 yards, then turn right along a permissive bridleway (a section of the Vanguard Way). As you approach a tarmac driveway, bear left along the bridleway, with a small wood to the left and a road to the right. As you near a main road, turn right, crossing an entrance drive, and going along a public footpath between hedgerows. Follow this path for about $^2/_3$ mile into Puplet Wood, with Selsdon Wood beyond the ditch to the left. This path ends when it reaches the main junction of tracks at the north-eastern corner of Selsdon Wood (the junction you crossed earlier): turn left, go through the gate and walk uphill, forking left after about 50 yards. Turn left again after a further 10 yards, following the path as it climbs steadily uphill through the woods. Where the path divides into three, follow the central track, keeping ahead at the next two path crossings.

Soon you reach a junction of five tracks: keep ahead and slightly left on the broad track, with a clearing to the right just beyond the trees. Keep ahead across another path and then go to the left of a wooden fence. At the crossing at the end of the fence, keep ahead, going slightly uphill. At the next crossing, turn right along a gravel track, following it out of the woods. Now go across the clearing to return to the car park, with Selsdon and the Selsdon Park Hotel on the hill ahead.

POINTS OF INTEREST:

Selsdon Wood – This nature reserve is a woodland bird sanctuary maintained by the National Trust. Many bird species can be found in the diverse woodland areas and the wood is famous for its bluebells. A carved wooden bear stands over the entrance to the car park.

REFRESHMENTS:

None on the route, but the woodland is a good place for a picnic.

Walks 50 & 51 HAMMERSMITH AND MORTLAKE $4\frac{3}{4}$m ($7\frac{1}{2}$km) or $6\frac{3}{4}$m (11km)

Maps: OS Sheets Landranger 176; Pathfinder 1175.
A towpath walk on both sides of the Thames.
Start: At 234785, Hammersmith Underground Station.

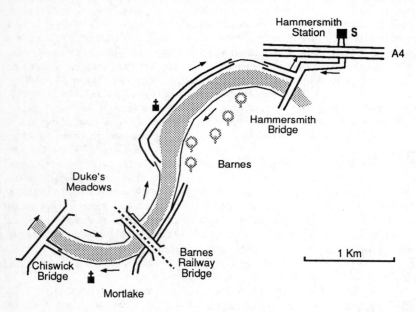

From Hammersmith Station look for exits to Fulham Palace Road and use the subway to go under the A4 flyover. Do not walk down Fulham Palace Road: instead, turn right to walk past the Hammersmith Apollo Theatre and through the car park, turning left down Hammersmith Bridge Road. Cross Hammersmith Bridge: the annual Oxford-Cambridge Boat Race starts from Putney Bridge and features the stretch of river you are about to walk along. At the end of the bridge, cross the road and walk westwards along the towpath towards Barnes and Chiswick. Follow this leafy towpath for nearly two miles to reach Barnes Railway Bridge. The path runs alongside Lonsdale Road as you pass Barnes High Street and approach the bridge.

The shorter walk goes up the steps to reach the footbridge on Barnes Railway Bridge. Cross the bridge and turn right to head back for Hammersmith on the Middlesex Bank of the Thames.

The longer walk goes under the bridge and continues along the towpath, passing Ye White Hart Inn. Follow the towpath towards Chiswick Bridge: shortly after the bridge comes into sight there is a plaque in a wall on the left showing the flood level of the Thames in 1928. From the Ship Tavern the post marking the finishing line for the Boat Race can be seen on the opposite bank. Go up the steps and cross **Chiswick Bridge**. Go right, down the steps and walk along the road between the Boat Clubhouse and the allotments. There is a grass track alongside the road all the way to the Chiswick Boathouse. Go to the left of the Boathouse and follow the road to the left, past Dukes Hollow Nature Reserve. A small detour away from the Thames is necessary here in order to avoid the railway: keep along the road and go under the railway bridge. Turn right and walk along the pavement of Riverside Drive. As the road bends left keep ahead on the pavement to rejoin the riverside path which is now followed to Barnes Railway Bridge where the shorter route is rejoined.

From Barnes Railway Bridge keep to the towpath, walking past a bandstand and playing fields. As you walk near a residential area the path-cycleway turns left and temporarily leaves the river in order to go round a newly developed area. Go around this area and turn right into Pumping Station Road. At the end of this road there is a small drive passing near St Nicholas's Church. Continue ahead on Chiswick Mall and **Hammersmith Terrace**. Walk to the right of the Black Lion – an inn has stood on this site for at least 200 years – to rejoin the riverside walk. Continue along the river path, passing the London Corinthian Sailing Club and a number of other interesting buildings. Walk through Furnival Gardens and pass more riverside inns, then at Hammersmith Bridge, turn left and follow the road round to the station.

POINTS OF INTEREST:
Chiswick Bridge – This is one of the river's more recent bridges, having been opened in 1933. It is the site of the finish of the Oxford-Cambridge Boat Race.
Hammersmith Terrace – This unassuming little street actually has much of interest. The terraced block was built in 1750 and there are three blue plaques to famous former residents. Black Lion Lane, adjoining, is infamous as the haunt of 'The Hammersmith Ghost'.

REFRESHMENTS:
The Ship Inn, Ship Lane, Mortlake.
The Black Lion, South Black Lion Lane, Hammersmith.

Walk 52　　　　**HYDE PARK**　　　　$4^3/_4$m ($7^1/_2$km)

Maps: OS Sheets Landranger 176; Pathfinder 1159 and 1175.
Pleasant parkland footpath walking.
Start: At 283798, Hyde Park Corner Underground Station.

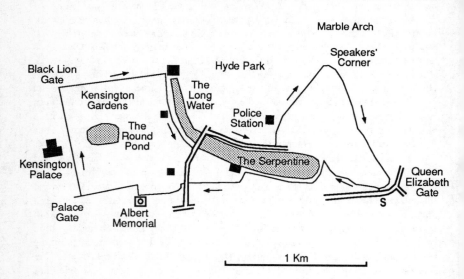

Leave Hyde Park Corner Station via exit 3 and use the pedestrian crossing to enter Hyde Park itself. The decorative Queen Elizabeth Gates, formally opened in 1993, and the Achilles Statue can be seen to the right. To begin the circuit of Hyde Park and Kensington Gardens, turn left to walk along Rotten Row, a prominent path and cycleway. After passing the Diana Statue, bear half-right along another tarmac path, heading for **The Serpentine**.

Walk towards the unusually-shaped Dell Restaurant building, then turn left to walk past the eastern end of the Serpentine. Follow the path known as 'Fisherman's Keep' along the southern edge of the lake to reach the Lido Pavilion. Here, turn left along the path, then right to rejoin Rotten Row.

Go across the road and through the small gate to enter Kensington Gardens: the Serpentine Gallery can be seen to the right. Once through the gate, keep left, heading for the **Albert Memorial**: the Royal Albert Hall can also be seen across Kensington Gore.

From a point directly north of the Albert Memorial (on the Kensington Gardens side), turn right, then almost immediately left, along 'The Flower Walk'. Go straight ahead along this, passing through another gate and continuing to reach public conveniences and the Palace Gate. Now turn right and walk along the Broad Walk, with Kensington Palace (and its State Apartments) to the left and the Round Pond to the right. After about $^1/_2$ mile, you will reach Black Lion Gate near the north-eastern corner of Kensington Gardens. Do not go through the gate: instead, turn right on to the path running along the northern edge of the park, parallel with the Bayswater Road. Follow this path for nearly $^1/_2$ mile to reach the Italian Water Gardens. Turn right and follow the path along the western edge of the Long Water, passing the delightful Peter Pan Statue, to reach the road, forking right just before the Serpentine Bridge.

At the road, turn left and cross the bridge. Now go left through an iron gate and left again along a small stone pathway. This descends, then turns to take the walker under the bridge and along the northern side of the Serpentine.

Walk past two boathouses and then take the broad path on the left, after Serpentine Lodge. Walk along this, slightly uphill, passing the Ranger's Lodge and the Royal Parks Constabulary Police Station. At the major junction of paths, bear half-right in the direction of Marble Arch and Speakers' Corner, crossing an area known as 'The Parade Ground'. On reaching the corner, turn right to follow the road close to the eastern boundary of Hyde Park, walking parallel with Park Lane. It is just over $^1/_2$ mile back to the Queen Elizabeth Gate and Hyde Park Corner Tube Station.

POINTS OF INTEREST:
The Serpentine – This famous lake attracts a wide variety of birds, including swans and herons. The Lido provides facilities for boating and swimming.
The Albert Memorial – Designed by Sir Gilbert Scott and completed in 1872, this famous memorial was repaired in 1994/95.

REFRESHMENTS:
The Dell Restaurant, The Serpentine.
The Orangery, Kensington Palace.

Walk 53   **HAMPSTEAD HEATH** $4^3/_4$m $(7^1/_2$km)

Maps: OS Sheets Landranger 176; Pathfinder 1159.

A mix of heathland, parks and streets.

Start: At 264858, Hampstead Underground Station.

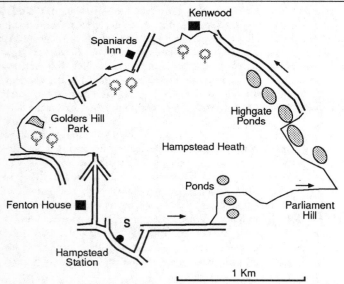

Leave Hampstead Station by the High Street exit and turn left. Opposite the Post Office, go left down Gayton Road. At the crossroads, turn right along Willow Road. Pass a section of heath and a play area and then turn left into Downshire Hill. Cross over and follow the road to the right of the car park. At the crossing of paths, with a pond ahead, do not go forward: instead, turn left along the cycleway. Follow the path between two ponds, continuing for about 100 yards before forking right to reach Parliament Hill. Shortly after reaching the summit, bear right along another stone path. Keep on this path, with a running track away to the right, until you reach the next junction. Now turn left, walk past the bandstand and cafe, and turn left (taking the right-hand fork, not the uphill path) to head towards Highgate Ponds.

   Continue along this broad path as it passes to the left of the first two ponds. After the second pond, bear right along a walkway. At the end of the fenced walkway, turn left to walk along the eastern edge of Highgate No. 3 Pond. At the end, turn right

106

and head uphill on the path next to the railed fence. Walk past the barrier and follow the track around to the left. Follow the track as it passes the Ladies Bathing Pond and eventually reaches an entrance gate to the Kenwood Estate in the fence on the left. Go through the gate, turn right and maintain direction towards **Kenwood House.**

Continue along the gravel drive by the South Front of the house. At the end of the house, turn right under a hedge archway and walk past the Garden Front. Shortly, turn left along a tarmac footpath (signposted 'Way Out'). Go through a 'Trellis Tunnel' to reach a car park and leave through the West Lodge Gate. Turn left along Hampstead Lane. The route now passes the Spaniards Inn at the top of the hill. Cross at the pedestrian crossing and take the downhill track beyond on to another section of heath. Continue along this track, ignoring all other paths. Pass to the right of two ponds and then, when a wooden fence appears ahead, bear right to pass a 'No Cycling' sign. Follow the tarmac path down to a road (North End). At the end, cross over and head uphill along a small, winding grass path. At the top, walk through the trees on the right, go down steps and through a gate into Golders Hill Park. Follow the path down past the cafe and Leg of Mutton Pond.

Continue past the end of the pond and, at the next crossing of paths, (after about 100 yards) turn left. Walk between the aviaries and the deer pen to reach an iron gate. Go through and turn right along a broad, gently inclining track, following it to a road. Turn left and go along the footpath running beside West Heath Road for about $^1/_4$ mile. Opposite a block of flats, bear left along the well-defined path going away from the road. Keep on this all the way up the hill to reach North End Way. Now turn right, cross Whitestone Walk, and follow the pavement to the left of the pond. Cross over and bear right slightly, over a pavement and down Hampstead Grove. You will soon pass Admiral's House and **Fenton House.** Shortly after the latter, go down an alleyway on the left and then turn right for the station.

POINTS OF INTEREST:

Kenwood House – This 17th-century House, with its landscaped park, contains the Iveagh Bequest, a collection of artworks left to the nation by the Earl of Iveagh.
Fenton House – This 17th-century National Trust property has a superb walled garden. Inside there are collections of ceramics and early musical instruments.

REFRESHMENTS:

The Brew House, Cafe and Garden, Kenwood.
Spaniards Inn, Hampstead Lane.

Walk 54   **TWICKENHAM**   4³/₄m (7¹/₂km)

Maps: OS Sheets Landranger 176; Pathfinder 1174.
Historic town streets, parks and riverside.
Start: At 161736, Twickenham Railway Station.

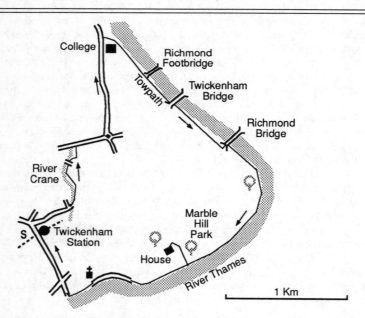

From the station forecourt, turn right and then right again at the roundabout. Almost immediately, turn right once more into Cole Park Road, a quiet residential street. After about 300 yards, between two white houses, an alleyway with a 'No Cycling' symbol appears on the right (ignore the first alleyway). Go down this, over a footbridge and turn left to walk alongside the River Crane in Cole Park. Bear left at the fence at the end of the children's play area and walk across the grass close to the river and a group of trees. Cross the road at Moor Mead Bridge and bear slightly right along a tarmac footpath to reach a road.

    Walk along the road and, at the first junction, turn left along Brook Road. (The route now follows roads for just under a mile to reach the Thames towpath near Isleworth.) At the main road turn right. Cross the footbridge and turn left at the roundabout. Walk along St Margaret's Road for about $^2/_3$ mile until you pass the Canada Gate of Brunel University College. Now turn right along Railshead Road to join the Thames towpath which is followed back to Twickenham.

The towpath shortly joins a road and passes Richmond footbridge: walk under the arches of Twickenham Bridge and the railway bridge on to a paved path called Ducks Walk. Continue past Richmond Bridge Mansions, and then turn left to approach Richmond Bridge itself. After about 30 yards, cross and go down steps to rejoin the towpath. After a further mile or so of pleasant towpath walking, **Marble Hill Park** appears on the right. Go through the black iron gate for a detour to Marble Hill House. The second path left takes you to the main entrance.

From the House, return to the riverside and resume the walk along the towpath. As you reach the western end of Marble Hill Park the riverside path passes through a gateway and goes to the left of a children's play area, with Ham House glimpsed across the river. At the end of the recreation ground, go along the diagonal path to reach a road. Turn left and follow the road past the White Swan Inn and under a footbridge which is part of the York House estate. (York House is a 17th-century mansion which is now occupied by Council Offices). The road passes to the left of **St Mary's Church**: follow the road beside the river with Twickenham Rowing Club visible on Eel Pie Island to the left and the Barmy Arms, complete with a reverse lettering pub sign, to the right.

Just before you are level with the footbridge to Eel Pie Island, leave the riverside by turning right down Water Lane. Cross King Street at the lights and continue down London Road to reach Twickenham Station.

POINTS OF INTEREST:

Marble Hill Park – Marble Hill House is a Thames-side Palladian Villa, built in 1729 for the Countess of Suffolk. It contains a collection of paintings and is now in the care of English Heritage.

St Mary's Church – The parish church of Twickenham dates mainly from 1714. Alexander Pope, the writer, is buried here. The church marks the original settlement of Twickenham. A plaque at the corner of Riverside and Church Lane records the level of the Thames in the flood of 1774.

REFRESHMENTS:

Coach House Cafe, Marble Hill Park.

There are also numerous possibilities in Twickenham, including those mentioned in the route description.

Maps: OS Sheets Landranger 176 or 177; Pathfinder 1140.
A fine walk on Country Park paths and bridleways.
Start: At 338985, the Forty Hall car park, Enfield.

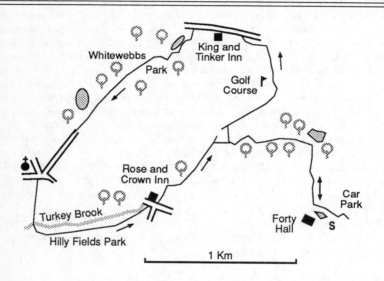

Go up the steps from the car park and turn right along a tarmac drive: a pond and
Forty Hall can be seen to the left. Just before the drive reaches two houses, turn right
at a metal gate. Walk past the information board and follow the grass path downhill.
After nearly $^1/_4$ mile the path enters a wooded section and then passes to the left of a
lake: ignore the right turns, keeping on the main track until it bends right near the end
of the wood and forms a T-junction with another prominent track. Turn left and walk
alongside Turkey Brook to reach a footbridge on the right.

Cross the footbridge, go over a stile and follow the well-defined path beyond,
with a wooden barrier fence on the right. After about 200 yards, divert left along a
smaller path. Go through/over a small wooden gate and turn right to join a metal-
fenced bridleway. Follow this bridleway for approximately $^1/_2$ mile, then, just before
reaching a road, turn left along a footpath next to the bridleway, following it along
the northern edge of the golf course. Shortly the path leaves the bridleway and continues

beside the road, passing the King and Tinker Inn which is said to have been visited by James I.

Follow the pavement to reach a roadside parking area and a wooden gated entrance to **Whitewebbs Park**. Turn left through the entrance and go along the tarmac drive. Turn right just before a metal gate to follow a path circling a lake. Turn left and walk beside the lake to its south-western end, then go left along a gravel track for about 20 yards before turning right along a small footpath into the woods (indicated by a wooden marker post). Where this path forks, keep right and, at post No. 11, turn left along a more clearly defined path. Follow the wooden post indicators until a set of wooden barriers appears to the right. Now walk through these and turn left along a bridleway. Follow the bridleway for about $1/2$ mile to emerge on to a road opposite the Fallow Buck Inn.

Cross and walk down Strayfield Road, passing to the left of St John's Church. Shortly, turn left along a tarmac footpath into Hilly Fields Park. After crossing a footbridge, fork left along another tarmac path. This path runs close to the brook for some distance and then reaches a junction next to another footbridge. Here leave the tarmac, continuing straight ahead on the grass. Walk to the right of a bandstand and, as you approach the eastern edge of the park, bear slightly right to converge with a tarmac path. Leave the park opposite the Rose and Crown Inn.

Cross Clay Hill and continue forward along a gravel path. After 100 yards, go left over a wooden footbridge and then immediately right along a path beside the brook. Keep right as this joins a bridleway close to a road. Ignore a footpath sign on the right (next to the golf course) and continue along the bridleway, with a stream to the right. After crossing two brooks, turn right off the bridleway, passing between metal barriers to join a rather overgrown footpath. At the end of this go right across a concrete footbridge. From this point retrace your outward steps back to the starting car park by following the path left and then turning right at the next major junction of tracks.

POINTS OF INTEREST:

Forty Hall – The Hall is an early 17th-century mansion previously occupied by a Lord Mayor of London. It is now a museum and art gallery.

Whitewebbs Park – The Park contains a mixture of woods, lakes and gardens. White Webbs House is now an old people's home.

REFRESHMENTS:

The King and Tinker, Whitewebbs Lane.

The Rose and Crown, Clay Hill.

111

Walk 56   CHELSEA AND BATTERSEA PARK   5m (8km)

Maps: OS Sheets Landranger 176; Pathfinder 1175.

A moderate Thames-side footpath walk.

Start: At 297784, Pimlico Underground Station.

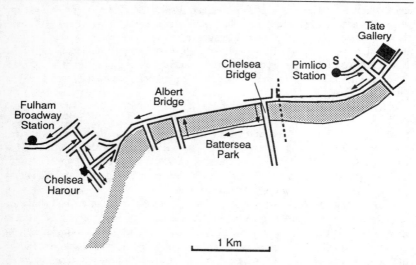

Leave Pimlico Station by the Bessborough Street North (Tate Gallery) exit. Walk to the traffic lights, cross the road and turn right to walk down Vauxhall Bridge Road. Turn left down John Islip Street: Millbrook Tower comes into view ahead. Walk past the Royal Army Medical College buildings and turn right into Atterbury Street. The Tate Gallery is now on your left. Cross Millbank and turn right. From this point the walk remains close to the Thames as far as Chelsea Harbour. Continue along Millbank and walk to the left of the bronze sculpture. Go up the steps, cross the road leading on to Vauxhall Bridge, and then go down the steps and along Crown Reach Riverside Walk, where there is an interesting mix of commercial and residential properties. Go through the gate at the end of the Riverside Walk and turn left to continue along Grosvenor Road.

Shortly, leave the road and go through a gate into Pimlico Gardens, where there is a statue of William Huskisson. There is an opportunity here to look at the Thames-side developments, both old and new, and the imposing structure of Battersea Power

112

Station (a listed building) can be seen on the other side of the river. Walk past the 'Westminster Boating Base' building and leave Pimlico Gardens by the gate to continue along Grosvenor Road. There is an interesting array of flats and tenements to the right, including the gigantic buildings of Dolphin Square. Walk along the embankment and under the railway bridge, then cross to the other side of the Thames by means of Chelsea Bridge. Turn right to enter **Battersea Park**. Keep to the riverside path, complete with old-fashioned lamp posts, and pass the 'Peace Pagoda', built by Buddhist monks and presented to London in 1985. There is an excellent view of the **Albert Bridge** from the western end of Battersea Park. Recross the Thames using the Albert Bridge, then turn left to walk along Chelsea Embankment. Across the road, on Cheyne Walk, is a statue of Thomas Carlyle (who lived near here) and the Kings Head and Eight Bells inns.

Continue ahead, still close to the river, along Cheyne Walk, to cross the road going on to Battersea Bridge. Now follow the footpath past the houseboats and on to Chelsea Wharf. As the road begins to go away from the river, turn left down Lots Road, following it as far as the mini-roundabout, where there is an inn called The Ferret and Firkin in a Ballon up the Creek. Turn left at the roundabout and walk along Chelsea Harbour Drive to visit the Harbour area. After the detour to the Harbour, complete the walk by first returning to the mini-roundabout and the Ferret and Firkin Inn. Continue north (ahead) along Lots Road to reach a T-junction with Kings Road. Turn right, cross the road via the zebra crossing and turn left at Hortensia Road, passing the buildings of King's College. Turn left along Fulham Road, following it past Stamford Bridge (Chelsea F.C.) to reach Fulham Broadway Station (District Line) from where the start can be regained.

POINTS OF INTEREST:

Battersea Park – The Park was created from marshland in 1853. In 1951 an amusement park was built here for the Festival of Britain. Nowadays the Park is once again more of a 'natural' environment, with a nature reserve, gardens and a lake.

The Albert Bridge – The bridge was opened in 1873 and is spectacularly illuminated at night. There is a notice at each end insisting "All troops must break step when marching over this bridge".

REFRESHMENTS:

The Kings Head and Eight Bells, Cheyne Walk, Chelsea.
The Ferret and Firkin, Lots Road, Chelsea Harbour.

Walk 57   UPMINSTER AND CRANHAM   5m (8km)

Maps: OS Sheets Landranger 177; Pathfinder 1160.
A mix of parks, rural footpaths and suburban streets.
Start: At 561869, Upminster Station (Rail and Underground).

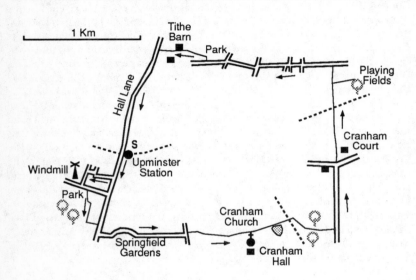

From the station forecourt, cross the road and turn left along Station Road. At Trinity
United Reform Church, turn right down Gaynes Road and, at the end, turn right along
Champion Road. Go left into Highview Gardens and left again down Cranbome
Gardens. On reaching St Mary's Lane, turn right to visit **Upminster Windmill**. Return
to St Mary's Lane and turn left, back towards Upminster and the church, passing
New Windmill Hall. Just before Gridiron Place, turn right along a tarmac footpath
into Upminster Park. Where this forks, keep right and walk to the southern edge of
the park. Turn left to reach the main road (Corbets Tey Road). Cross at the pelican
crossing and turn right. Turn left down Springfield Gardens, following this suburban
road for nearly $\frac{1}{2}$ mile to reach a T-junction with Argyle Gardens. Turn left, then
right along a footpath signposted to Cranham Church. Go through a gate and continue
along the footpath beside the hedgerow to reach All Saints Church. The footpath

continues through the churchyard and is signposted 'Pike Lane $^1/_2$m'. Walk around the Church to look at the buildings of Cranham Hall, then go over the stile near the north-eastern corner of the churchyard. The path beyond slopes gently downhill, with the M25 motorway visible in the distance. Continue ahead, across the fields, going to the left of a pond and go under the railway line. Now head half-right across a field towards the corner with the woods. Go through a gap in the trees and turn right, and then left, guided by the posts with yellow arrows, to reach Pike Lane.

Turn left along the lane for just under $^1/_2$ mile to reach a T-junction (the Thatched House Inn is just to the left). Go straight over St Mary's Lane and along the footpath to the left of Cranham Court. The path goes along the edge of a field and between hedgerows to reach the Fenchurch Street to Shoeburyness railway line. Go over the large metal stile and cross the line with care. Now follow the left-hand edge of Cranham Playing Fields and then a grass track to reach a smaller recreation ground and car park at the end of Sunnycroft Gardens. On entering the car park, turn immediately left to walk along Limerick Gardens. Go over at a crossroads and continue straight ahead along Kings Gardens. At the T-junction with Front Lane, turn left and almost immediately right up steps into Brookmans Close. At the end of the Close, turn left and immediately right up Esdale Gardens. About halfway along Esdale Gardens, on the right, there is a driveway into Upminster Hall Playing Fields. Go down this drive and turn left to walk through the park, keeping to the left of the changing rooms and walking beside the children's play area. **Upminster Tithe Barn** is ahead: Upminster Hall, the white building nearby, is now the Clubhouse for Upminster Golf Club (and private property). Leave Upminster Tithe Barn and turn left down Hall Lane. The Ingrebourne Valley can be seen beyond the golf course to the right. You may also be able to see the spire of St Andrew's Church, Hornchurch, in the distance. Continue down Hall Lane for about $^1/_2$ mile to return to Upminster Station.

POINTS OF INTEREST:
Upminster Windmill – This eight-sided, white clapboard, smock windmill was completed in 1802. It was in operation for 100 years before it fell into disuse. It is now in the care of the Hornchurch and District Historical Society.

Upminster Tithe Barn – The Barn houses an Agricultural and Folk Museum containing a collection of items from bygone times. On certain days of the year it is open to the public.

REFRESHMENTS:
There are many refreshment possibilities in the centre of Upminster, particularly on Station Road and Corbets Tey Road.

Maps: OS Sheets Landranger 176; Pathfinder 1190.
Historic gardens, parkland and a towpath.
Start: At 151689, the car park next to Hampton Court Green.

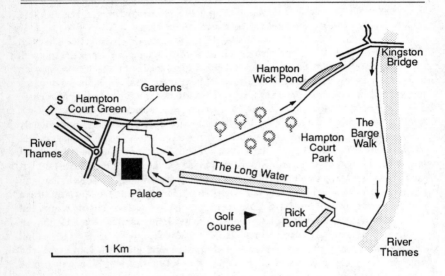

Leave the car park along the gravel track going diagonally across Hampton Court
Green. On reaching the far corner of the Green, cross Hampton Court Road and
continue along the tree-lined pavement. After about 200 yards, turn right through the
red-brick gateway to enter **Hampton Court Gardens** (there is an admission fee for
Hampton Court Palace, but the gardens and park are free).

   Turn left immediately, passing the 300 year-old Maze on your right and the
Lion Gate on your left (the Lion Gate entrance to Bushy Park is across the road).
Continue along Laburnum Walk, turning left immediately after the Ladies' Public
Conveniences to follow a path along the walled edge of the gardens to reach a green
gate on the left. Go through the gate into the Fountain Garden. Walk ahead, then turn
right and left along gravel paths to reach a bridge. Cross the bridge and go through
the ornate iron gates signposted to the 20th-Century Garden. Walk along the broad

tree-lined avenue across Hampton Court Park for just over $^1/_2$ mile: the tower of Kingston Church can be seen in the distance straight ahead and you may see deer in the open spaces of the park. At the end of the trees, bear slightly left to walk along the edge of Hampton Wick Pond. Leave Hampton Court Park by the Kingston Gate. Turn right, but before reaching Kingston Bridge, turn right again along **The Barge Walk**. After nearly a mile of towpath walking, level with the end of Raven's Ait, there is a small iron gate on the right: go through to re-enter Hampton Court Park. Now walk along the fenced grass path, go through the next gate and walk to the edge of Rick Pond. Turn right and walk around the north-eastern end of the pond, then leave the water along a grass path, following it to a tarmac drive: Hampton Court Palace can be seen again in the distance. At the crossroads, continue forwards, walking on the grass between the drive and Long Water, with the Palace still directly ahead.

Walk beside the water for just over $^1/_2$ mile, then, as you approach the gardens, follow the fence round to the left, go through the iron gate, cross the footbridge and continue straight ahead along the broad gravel drive to the Palace. At the East Front of the Palace, turn right and, at the end of the buildings, go left to pass through the green gate you went through earlier. Now continue forward to reach a T-junction of paths. Turn right, and after about 100 yards turn left and go through the doorway in a red-brick wall (signposted Tiltyard Restaurant). Turn left again and walk past the restaurant and shop buildings. Continue forwards, going through the archway ahead to reach the front entrance area to the Palace (one wing was badly damaged by fire in 1986, but has since been restored). Walk across the forecourt and through the gate to reach the Thames path. Turn right and walk towards Hampton Court Bridge, designed by Lutyens. At the bridge, turn right, crossing the road by using the crossing. Turn left at the roundabout, cross over and walk along the southern edge of the Green to return to the starting car park.

POINTS OF INTEREST:

Hampton Court Gardens – The Palace, with its centuries of history, is, of course, enormously popular, but the Gardens and the Park are worth a visit in their own right. Attractions include the Maze (admission fee) and the Great Vine.

The Barge Walk – There has been a riverside path here since the time of King Henry VIII. The towpath extends $2^1/_2$ miles from Kingston Bridge to Hampton Court Bridge.

REFRESHMENTS:

Garden Cafe and Restaurant, Hampton Court Gardens.
The Cardinal Wolsey, Hampton Court Road.

Walk 59   EALING AND GUNNERSBURY   5m (8km)

Maps: OS Sheets Landranger 176; Pathfinder 1158 and 1174.
A walk through parks, greens and streets.
Start: At 179809, Ealing Broadway Underground Station.

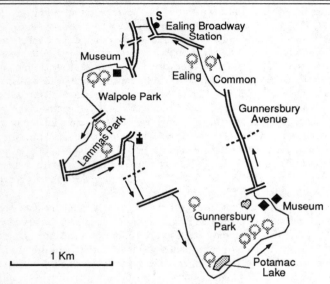

From the Station exit, go straight across the Broadway, walk past the delicatessen and along the pavement on the left side of Haven Green. At the far side of the green, turn left, go over the railway bridge, cross the Broadway once more and continue down High Street, with the Shopping Centre on your left. At the end, use the pedestrian crossing (50 yards after the mini-roundabout) to cross Ealing Green Street. Now cross Ealing Green along the tarmac footpaths to reach a gate. Go through to reach **Pitshanger Manor Museum**. From the Museum exit, turn left and left again to enter Walpole Park. Follow the path by the northern fence and, at the next gate, bear left with the tarmac path, going along the park's western edge. Shortly after passing the tennis courts, turn right and leave through the Lammas Park Gardens gate.

Turn right, cross Culmington Road and walk down Elers Road for a few yards to enter Lammas Park. Turn right and follow the footpath, keeping to the right-hand side of the park and passing a children's play area to reach its western end. At the road, turn left and then go left again along Windermere Road. Follow the road for about ¹/₃ mile as it becomes Lothair Road and ends at a T-junction. Cross and turn left at the junction, then follow the road as it curves right. At St Mary's Church, turn right to walk bewteen the church and the Rose and Crown Inn. At the end of the road, turn right along a paved alleyway (Robert's Alley), following it as it crosses the railway. Now continue along Olive Road to reach the Gunnersbury Tavern. Turn left and walk past a parade of shops. Cross Lionel Road and enter Gunnersbury Park. Keep right to walk along the western edge for about ¹/₂ mile, then, at the far corner, go around the fenced Potomac Pond and pass a ruined tower. Keep right after this, walking along the southern perimeter path for another ¹/₂ mile or so, with a cemetery on your right. At the park's south-eastern corner, follow the tarmac path as it curves left and passes a gate. The path curves left once more and then forks: take the right branch and, at the crossing of paths, go ahead to arrive between the two large white buildings. A plaque under the archway commemorates the opening of the park in 1926 by Neville Chamberlain. The building on the left is the **Gunnersbury Park Museum**: walk to the right of it, then turn left to pass the museum entrance. Keep on this drive to reach the exit by the North Lodge.

Cross Pope's Lane and walk to the right of Barons Pond, down Gunnersbury Drive. Follow the road as it converges with the main road (Gunnersbury Avenue). Shortly after crossing the railway, Ealing Common appears on the left: cross this using the diagonal tarmac footpath to reach a road. Cross and roughly maintain direction across the grass beyond to reach the far corner of the Common. Turn left along the main road (Uxbridge Road) and follow it for about ¹/₃ mile to reach Ealing Broadway. For the station, turn right at the main traffic lights.

POINTS OF INTEREST:

Pitshanger Manor Museum – The Manor House on Ealing Green is now owned by the local council but was once the property of Spencer Walpole, the politician. It now houses a museum and a public library.

Gunnersbury Park Museum – The museum houses a number of interesting exhibits. The buildings date from the 19th century, but there has been a manor house here since at least the 15th century. The house was previously in the possession of the Rothschild family.

REFRESHMENTS:

The North Star, Ealing Broadway.

There is a cafeteria at Gunnersbury Park (near the museum).

Walk 60   WANSTEAD PARK   5m (8km)

Maps: OS Sheets Landranger 177; Pathfinder 1160.
A walk through East London Parks.
Start: At 436865, Ilford Railway Station.

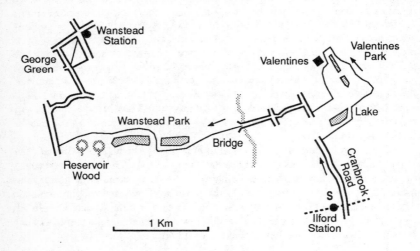

From Ilford Station cross over, turn left and walk along the busy Cranbrook Road. After about ¹/₄ mile, shortly after crossing Park Avenue, you will reach a green-gated entrance to Valentine's Park on the right. Go through the gate and take the central footpath to reach the edge of the lake. Turn right and walk along the broad tarmac footpath, signposted to Melbourne Field, by the lake. Bear left to walk around the north-eastern end of the lake, cross a small bridge and keep ahead to reach the cafeteria and a signpost. From the signpost continue in the direction of Perth Road. After about 200 yards, turn left along a footpath beside a small stream with a small green railed fence by it. Keep along this path as it crosses the stream by means of a small wooden bridge and then continue ahead on the path signposted to the Miniature Golf Course. Where this joins further paths, keep left and walk around the eastern side of the pond. Cross another small bridge and then turn right to walk along the nearside of an oblong-shaped pond. Follow the path parallel with the pond until you reach a path to the left, just before the end of the water. Now walk towards the tennis courts, turn left and then, after about 100 yards, turn right into a garden with hedges and palm trees. Leave this garden by the arch in the wall at the right-hand corner, passing a small aviary to reach **Valentine's Mansion**.

From the Mansion, head back towards the centre of the park. Cross a small wooden bridge and immediately turn right along a path that curves left and then runs beside the western perimeter fence. Ignore the exit gates at Mayors Avenue and Holcombe Road, continuing to the tennis courts. Turn right along the path to a gate: the cricket ground is to the left. Go through, cross Cranbrook Road at the pedestrian crossing and turn right. Turn left down Clarendon Gardens. At the end, cross, go right for a few yards, and then left down Highlands Gardens. At the bottom (by St John's Church), turn right and then left through the black iron gate into **Wanstead Park**. Cross the footbridge over the North Circular Road and go over the smaller of the two bridges over the River Roding. At a T-junction of paths, bear left to reach a fork. Take the left branch, following this main path to the left of Perch Pond. At the Wanstead Park Avenue Gate, turn right along the edge of Heronry Pond. At the kiosk, turn left and follow the path along the northern edge of the pond, keeping left, close to the water, at the next noticeboard. As you approach the end of Heronry Pond, bear right slightly to go along a well-defined path that takes you around the northern end of Shoulder of Mutton Pond and into Reservoir Wood, with the Golf Course to your right. Upon leaving the wood, turn right and walk along Blake Hall Road to the traffic lights. Now turn right and walk along Overton Drive to reach Draycot Road on the left. Walk along Draycot Road until George Green appears: there were protests against the construction of the M11 link road here in 1994. Go diagonally across the green to reach Wanstead Underground Station. From here Central Line trains will take you to Stratford, and from there the Liverpool Street line will return you to Ilford.

POINTS OF INTEREST:

Valentine's Mansion – The building provides a focal point in the northern section of the park. The house is used by the council and is not open to the public, but there are pleasant gardens and ponds nearby.

Wanstead Park – Originally, in the 18th century, the park included formal gardens and Wanstead House, but it is now fairly wild and open.

REFRESHMENTS:

The George Inn, Wanstead.
The cafeteria in Valentine's Park.

Walk 61   **BANSTEAD DOWNS**   5m (8km)

Maps: OS Sheets Landranger 176 or 187; Pathfinder 1191.

A circuit on country paths and bridleways.

Start: At 276612, the car park at The Oaks Park, off the A2022, Croydon Lane, between Banstead and Purley.

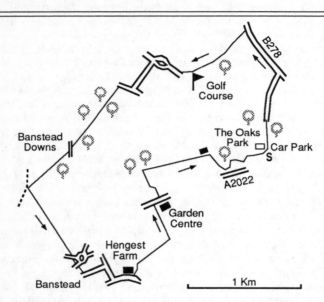

Head north from the car park (away from the A2022) on the main drive through **The Oaks** Park (this passes close to the cafe and has a 'No Through Road' sign). Walk past the white barrier on a wide gravel drive going slightly downhill, with a golf course to the left (behind the hedge) and an open expanse of downland to the right.

At the end of the drive, walk past another white barrier and a house, and then turn left along the permissive footpath (not the bridleway) signposted to Carshalton Beeches. This path is part of the 'Sutton Countryside Walk' and runs close to the B278 road. After about ¹/₄ mile the path reaches a wooden gate at Fox Hole Corner: turn left along another well-defined path to reach a triangle of grass called 'Woodpecker Triangle'. There, fork right, leaving the Sutton Countryside Walk. Now ignore a path to the right, going up a small bank and continuing on the track along the northern edge of the golf course. Shortly after this enters an area of undergrowth, bear right through the trees and up a set of steps to reach a gravel drive going uphill. Continue along the unmade residential road, bearing left at the end into Pine Walk, and then left again at Fairway. At the end, turn right and then, after about 100 yards, go left along the public bridleway opposite Banstead Road South.

Stay on the bridleway as it crosses a road. Later, where it forks, keep right. Now go straight across the next road (Sutton Lane) on to Banstead Downs, bearing left along a grass track almost immediately after passing the barrier next to the road. Ignore a minor path to the left, staying on the track until it goes downhill and reaches a railway bridge. Do not cross the bridge: instead, take the second track on the left (not the path closest to the railway), following it as it climbs gently uphill to reach a signposted footpath-bridleway crossing. Go straight across, keeping on the hedged bridleway. Follow this green lane between back gardens for about $^1/_3$ mile to reach a road near a roundabout. Cross and continue along the small tarmac drive, repeating this procedure at the next road. When the path reaches an area of green in a residential road, bear left along the pavement.

At the end of this suburban avenue, turn right, and at the end of the street cross and go left to reach Hengest Farm. Cross over again and follow the hedged public footpath close to the farm entrance. The path skirts the right-hand and top edges of a large field to reach an almost hidden stile in the far corner. Go over and follow the footpath beyond, continuing along a track between the farm buildings and a large garden centre to reach Croydon Lane. Cross the road and walk right, along it, for about 100 yards to reach a signed public footpath on the left. Follow this until it meets another path in a small wooded area. At this point, turn right and follow the well-defined bridleway for $^1/_3$ mile to reach a farm. Turn right at the farm road and walk past Fairlawn Cottage to approach Croydon Lane once more. Turn left just before the lane, going along a permissive bridleway. It is now just $^1/_2$ mile back to the car park and refreshments at The Oaks Park, with a choice of footpath or bridleway for the final $^1/_4$ mile!

POINTS OF INTEREST:
The Oaks – Near the entrance to the Park some fallen trees have been left in 'Memory of the Storm'. There is also a craft centre, a nature trail and picnic areas.

REFRESHMENTS:
The Parks Cafe, The Oaks Parks.

Walk 62   KEW RIVERSIDE   5¼m (8½km)

Maps: OS Sheets Landranger 176; Pathfinder 1174.
Pleasant walking on towpaths, parkland and streets.
Start: At 192768, Kew Gardens Underground Station.

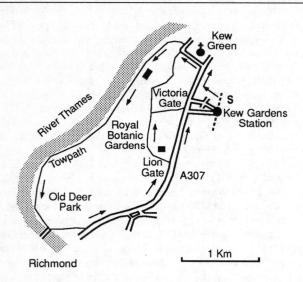

The walk described here is a circuit of the Royal Botanical Gardens in Kew, including about 2½ miles of Thames towpath. The route does not actually enter the gardens but does pass several entrances. An alternative is to follow the route as far as the Lion Gate and then make your way north through the gardens to leave by either the Victoria Gate or the main entrance near Kew Green. This provides an interesting alternative to the final street section of the walk, but you have to be willing to pay the entrance fee!

From the station forecourt, bear right down Station Approach. Cross the road at the junction and continue along Broomfield Road. This reaches Kew Road, with the wall of Kew Gardens ahead. Cross and turn right to walk beside the wall. At the traffic lights, bear left, and then keep left again into Kew Green. Now walk with the Green and St Anne's Church to your right, until you pass the main entrance to the **Royal Botanic Gardens**.

124

Follow the road around to the right for about 200 yards and then turn left down Ferry Lane. At the end, turn left along the Thames towpath, which is now followed for about $2^1/_2$ miles. Shortly, the red-bricked Kew Palace can be seen to the left. After passing the car park and the Brentford Ferry Gate the towpath affords occasional glimpses of the exotic plants and trees in the gardens to the left and there is a good view of Syon House across the river.

Further on the towpath reaches Richmond Lock and Footbridge. Just after the bridge, go left across a much smaller footbridge into the **Old Deer Park** Recreation Ground. Follow the tarmac path until it joins the Twickenham Road. Now walk past the swimming baths and Richmond Athletic Ground and, at the large roundabout, keep left along the pavement to walk past a row of shops on Kew Road. The road passes another sports ground – the home of both London Welsh Rugby Club and Richmond Cricket Club – and offers a view of the Pagoda in Kew Gardens. Follow the road past the Lion Gate, from where the alternative finish to the route starts, continuing along the road for a further $^1/_2$ mile. On reaching the Victoria Gate, cross over and go up Lichfield Street back to Station Parade.

POINTS OF INTEREST:

Royal Botanic Gardens – Allow several hours for a full exploration of the site's 300 acres. There are plants and trees from all over the world and displays at the visitor centre (Victoria Gate) illustrate the research and conservation functions of the Gardens. There is a new Evolution House and famous buildings include the Palm House, the Pagoda and Kew Palace.

Old Deer Park – The Old Deer Park by the river is neither as spectacular nor as large as Richmond Park further south. It does, however, contain a range of sports faciltites and is home to the annual Richmond Horse Show.

REFRESHMENTS:

The Flower and Firkin, Free House, Kew Gardens Station.
Kew Greenhouse Cafe, Station Parade.
The Orangery, Royal Botanical Gardens.

Walk 63   ADDINGTON HILLS   5¹/₄m (8¹/₂km)

Maps: OS Sheets Landranger 187 or 177; Pathfinder 1191.
A fairly demanding hill and wood trail.
Start: At 328643, Croydon South Rail Station.

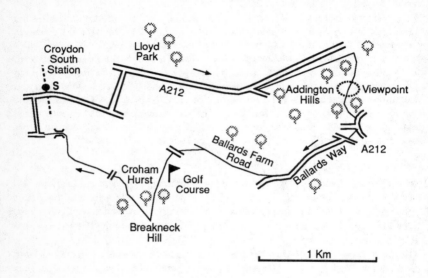

From the station exit, turn left to walk through the car park and then go down a flight
of steps. Turn left along Croham Road, following it for about ¹/₃ mile to reach Campden
Road on the left. Walk up this, turning right at the end. Though still in suburbia, you
are now on the Vanguard Way – a long distance footpath from Croydon to East Sussex.
After about 100 yards, cross and go up six steps to enter Lloyd Park. Turn right and
walk along the edge of the Park closest to the road. Walk across the car park and
maintain direction along the tarmac footpath between the Park and the road. Keep on
this as it climbs gradually and passes the entrance to Coombe Lodge. Cross Oaks
Road and turn left. Now walk to the left of the car park to enter the **Addington Hills**
area, keeping to the footpath nearest to Oaks Road. At a small triangular clearing
with two trees, keep left. Do not stray to the right – it is easy to get lost on the Addington
Hills! Shortly the path forks: bear left towards the road and then curve right to walk

parallel with the road, but about 10 yards away from it. Ignore a path to the right, maintaining your easterly direction on the path close to the road. Shortly, at another fork, keep left along the smaller, more overgrown path. Where this joins another path, keep left again. Soon the path dips and then reaches a T-junction: turn right to finally walk away from Oaks Road and to begin heading over Addington Hills.

Follow the stony path as it takes you to the top of a hill and then levels out as a broader track. Walk along the plateau, passing two items of a fitness track to join another gravel track. Turn right and walk towards the car park next to the restaurant. Turn left and walk through the car park and along the entrance road. Cross the road and turn right. At Bishops Walk, recross the road and follow the footpath near the bus stop. Cross the A212, with care, and walk along Ballards Way. Soon this goes downhill quite steeply and a section of Bramley Bank Nature Reserve can be seen to the left. Cross Hollingsworth Road and, where Ballards Way curves left, continue straight on along Ballards Farm Road (another section of the Vanguard Way). Keep on this undulating bridleway for $^1/_2$ mile, forking left at a green lamp-post. At the road, cross and walk along the drive to Croham Hurst Golf Club. Join the footpath to the right of the clubhouse and follow it into **Croham Hurst** to reach the top of the ominously-named Breakneck Hill, ignoring a crossing path as you enter the main part of the woods beside a ditch.

As you reach the top of the hill, the route goes sharp right along a gravel path, but do take time to explore the hilltop area. The downhill path brings you to a road called Bankside: turn left, cross Croham Manor Wood and head along the broad, fenced footpath opposite Bankside. Follow this path as it passes the Emmanuel Parish Church and continue down Rockhampton Road. Bear right after passing the school and keep ahead along the pavement at the end of the close to cross a footbridge. Go down the steps and continue under two bridges, turning right into St Peters Road. The steps to Croydon South Station are across the road at the end of this street.

POINTS OF INTEREST:

Addington Hills – The route includes a semi-circuit of these hills which provide an important recreational area between Croydon and Selsdon. There is a viewpoint on the eastern hill.

Croham Hurst – There is a good view from the top of the hill. A plaque marks the site of a Bronze Age round barrow.

REFRESHMENTS:

None on the route, the nearest being in South Croydon.

Walk 64   MONKEN HADLEY   5¹/₄m (8¹/₂km)

Maps: OS Sheets Landranger 176; Pathfinder 1140.

Visiting Monken Hadley Common and village.

Start: At 250962, High Barnet Underground Station.

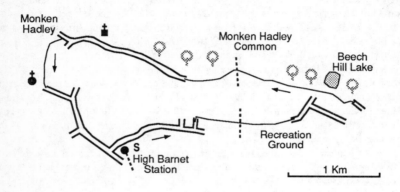

Leave the station, turn right and walk up the hill. At the lights, turn right along Meadway. After about ¹/₂ mile, at the first major junction, follow Potters Road around to the left, passing St Mark's Church. About 300 yards further on, turn left into Clifford Road and, after following it for 30 yards, go right along a tarmac footpath. Ignore two paths going right, keeping ahead across a road and going under the railway to reach a recreation ground. Follow the path just inside the left-hand edge of the recreation ground and, shortly after passing a children's play area, go left through a gateway and immediately right to continue along a road. At the end of the road (Lawton Road) cross and use the footbridge over Pymme's Brook. Turn left and walk on the grass beside the brook for about 250 yards before turning right into Linthorpe Road. At the end, cross Northfield Road and continue along a tarmac footpath which will bring you out to a road at the eastern end of **Monken Hadley Common**.

Turn left along the road to begin the return journey to High Barnet. Walk past the Middlesex University Conference Centre and follow the footpath marked as part of the Pymme's Brook Trail. The main path through the trees takes the walker gently downhill and across a small brick bridge: at the three-way signpost, keep ahead, in the direction of Hadley and High Barnet. (**Beech Hill Lake**, just to the right of this point, provides a pleasant resting spot). The track turns to tarmac as it gradually ascends Newman's Hill and crosses the railway: walk past the car park and the Pymme's Brook Trail noticeboard (this is a starting point for the trail). Follow the path along the edge of the Common, then continue along the road to reach the junction of Bakers Hill and Hadley Common. Walk ahead on the grass to the right of the road and, after passing a red-brick mansion called 'Priddeons', cross and continue along the verge on the other side of the road. Monken Hadley Church stands at the western end of the Common.

Walk past the Rectory and go through the white gate. Cross, walk past the church entrance and go along Dury Road, with the village ponds to your left. Pass a number of cottages and, at the junction with Hatfield Road (the Old Windmill Inn is a short distance to the right), cross and maintain direction across the grass. Walk to the left of a small, overgrown pond to reach a junction of paths close to several sections of wooden fence. Do not take the first path on the left: instead, go forward past the wooden post and then bear left along the path passing between back gardens and several allotments. Continue by a golf course and, at the houses, keep ahead along the cycleway. Cross Hadley Grove and keep ahead along Christ Church Passage. At the road, turn left and then bear right at the lights to go along Barnet High Street, following it to return to High Barnet Station.

POINTS OF INTEREST:

Monken Hadley Common – The Common was once part of Enfield Chase, a vast tract of woodland north of London used for hunting. Some areas of the Common are reserved as grazing land and a number of local people have retained the right to graze livestock. The white gates around the Common are 'listed buildings'.

Beech Hill Lake – Great Crested Grebes and Common Terns are regularly seen at the lake, now used mainly for fishing. Locally the lake is known as 'Jack's Lake' because it was constructed for Mr Charles Jack of Beech Hill House around 1880.

REFRESHMENTS:

The Old Windmill Inn, Monken Hadley.
Ye Olde Mitre Inne, Barnet High Street.

Walk 65   RODING VALLEY   5¼m (8½km)

Maps: OS Sheets Landranger 177; Pathfinder 1141.
An easy riverside and park stroll.
Start: At 409918, Woodford Underground Station.

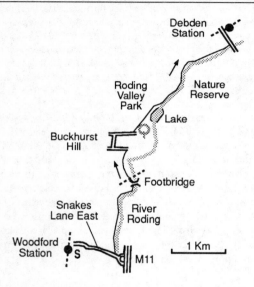

Leave Woodford Station from the westbound platform (use the subway just outside the station exit if you have travelled from central London) and walk along Snakes Lane East to the traffic lights. Continue along Snakes Lane East for a further ¹/₃ mile to reach a roundabout. Bear left and, just before the M11 road bridge, turn left through an entrance to Roding Valley Park. Walk along the path by the river and, after about ¹/₃ mile, walk past a footbridge to reach the northern end of Ray Park.

A sign ahead, next to the motorway, indicates that you are about to enter Essex. The grass track beside the river contributes to making this a green and 'rural' route, though the sounds of trains and cars provide frequent reminders that the walker is still not very far away from the metropolis.

Just before the river reaches a railway bridge, cross using a small footbridge and continue along the west bank, passing underneath the arches carrying the Central Line: this section of the route follows the edge of a sports field and a tarmac path passing allotments and garages. Beyond the garages, keep right along a tarmac path that converges with the river once more. As the path passes more allotments, the River Roding curves away to the right and a diversion is required before the river is rejoined further north. Go through an iron gate and walk along the road past a school. About halfway along the road, turn right into Alfred Road. At the end, cross, turn right and, shortly after crossing Rous Road, enter **Roding Valley Park** and Nature Reserve on the left. Follow the surfaced path past a children's playground and, where the path passes between trees and the corner of an allotment, bear half-right across the grass towards an information board next to the boating lake.

From the board, follow the path along the near (western) edge of the lake. Where the path diverts left, keep forward on the grass, going around the northern end of the lake to meet the River Roding once more. The river curves left and then right, and another path leads to a small wooden footbridge over Loughton Brook. The path beyond follows the river left and right again and then reaches a footbridge which leads into the Nature Reserve. Do not cross this bridge: instead, continue along the riverside path, bearing right at the next junction of paths to cross the Debden Brook. The gravel path now continues through Great Horsley Meadow to reach a gate next to Loughton Bridge: turn left and walk along Chigwell Lane for about $^1/_4$ mile to reach Debden Station from where Central Line underground trains will return you to the start.

POINTS OF INTEREST:
Roding Valley Park – It is encouraging to see how the river valley has in parts been developed for recreational purposes. The park area west of Buckhurst Hill and Loughton, with sports pitches and a boating lake, is particularly popular. The Nature Reserve is situated to the east of the river and is accessed via the Charlie Moule Bridge.

REFRESHMENTS:
The Railway Tavern, Snakes Lane East, Woodford.

Walk 66   BEDDINGTON PARK $5\frac{1}{4}$m ($8\frac{1}{2}$km)

Maps: OS Sheets Landranger 176; Pathfinder 1191.
Ponds, parkland and the River Wandle.
Start: At 277649, Carshalton Railway Station.

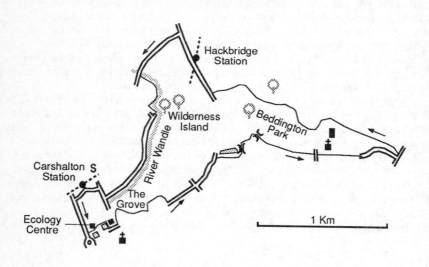

From the main station exit, turn right and walk down the hill. At the bottom turn left along West Street. After nearly $\frac{1}{4}$ mile, shortly before a roundabout, turn left along Festival Walk, passing **Sutton Ecology Centre**. Continue along Honeywood Walk, to the left of a pond, cross over and walk to the right of the second pond on the High Street. At the end of the pond, turn left to enter The Grove. At the junction of paths, go left for a few yards, and then right along a broad concrete walkway to the right of a stretch of water. Follow the walkway as it passes under a weeping willow and then curves right. Go to the left of a play area and, as you approach the buildings, turn left. Go left again along another path between the tennis court and a clubhouse. Go past a trim track and over a bridge to reach Westcroft Leisure Centre. Turn right and walk along the access road for about 100 yards, then bear left down a quiet residential street which has been closed to traffic at this end. At the far end, cross and continue along London Road. Shortly after crossing Derek Avenue, turn right into a car park for **Beddington Park**. Walk along the path between Grange Lake and the Play Centre, go over a footbridge and turn right. Go right over the next bridge and continue along the tarmac path beyond for nearly $^1/_2$ mile to meet a road close to St Mary's Church.

Walk to the right of the churchyard, following Church Path and Church Lane. Keep ahead as the lane becomes a residential road and, at the end, bear left to go downhill. At a main road, turn left and immediately left again along a paved path to begin the return journey to Carshalton. Go right over the wooden footbridge and then follow the left-hand path close to the river. Where this tarmac path veers right at a fence, keep ahead along a gravel path and then follow the diagonal path across a meadow. At the corner, cross a stream (Carew Manor Education Centre can be seen ahead and left) and go diagonally across a field to reach a car park. Walk past the car park barrier and along the entrance road. Where this forms a T-junction, bear left along the curving drive in front of Beddington Park Cottages. As this passes a black and white building dated 1877, keep right along another tarmac drive which takes you over a stone bridge and then past a play area and a cafe. The drive now curves left and follows the northern edge of the park to reach London Road.

Cross, with care, and turn right. Go over the railway close to Hackbridge Station and, shortly, turn left along Hackbridge Road, following it for nearly $^1/_4$ mile to reach a bridge. At the end of the green fence, turn left along the cycleway signposted to Carshalton. Keep left on the path close to the river and, shortly after passing Watermill House, at a road, turn left. This road (River Gardens) passes an entrance to **Wilderness Island**. Continue along Mill Lane until it reaches a crossroads with North Street. Now turn right to return to Carshalton Station.

POINTS OF INTEREST:

Sutton Ecology Centre – This innovatory centre contains displays on recycling, alternative energy sources, organic gardening and much else of ecological interest.
Beddington Park – A Heritage Trail provides details of the Park's history. St Mary's Church and Carew Manor are located in the eastern section of the park.
Wilderness Island – This London Wildlife Trust Nature Reserve is enclosed by a railway and two arms of the River Wandle. Over 70 species of wildflower have been recorded here.

REFRESHMENTS:

The Lord Palmerston, Mill Lane, Carshalton.
The Parks Cafe, The Grove.

Maps: OS Sheets Landranger 176; Pathfinder 1139.
A walk through Harefield village and along the Grand Union Canal towpath.
Start: At 052906, the crossroads at Harefield Village Green.

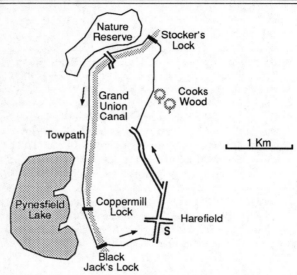

From the crossroads at the centre of **Harefield**, walk northwards along Rickmansworth Road for about 400 yards and then fork left along Hill End Road. Stay on this road for about $\frac{2}{3}$ mile, passing Harefield Hospital, the Plough Inn and Cripps House Farm. Leave the road by crossing a stile to the right of Cripps Farm Bungalow. Follow the hedged grass track beyond and, shortly, bear right at a public footpath sign next to a double wooden gate. The path skirts the edge of Cooks Wood: at the end of the wood cross a wooden barrier and maintain direction along the left-hand side of a large sloping field, as indicated by the yellow arrow. Towards the end the path curves right with the field boundary: go over a stile and then left along a track. Walk to the right of Stocker's Farm and then go left through the car parking area behind the buildings to reach a bridge over the Grand Union Canal at Stocker's Lock. The route now follows the canal towpath for about 2$\frac{1}{2}$ miles.

At the end of the bridge at Stocker's Lock, go right over the metal barrier and down the steps. Immediately, turn right again, going under the bridge to commence the canalside return journey westwards, and then southwards, to Harefield. Soon, **Stocker's Lake Nature Reserve** is to your right and a signpost just beyond the bridge at Springwell Lock indicates that you are walking in the direction of Coppermill Lock. The lock is reached after a further $1^1/_4$ miles of towpath walking. Go under Bridge 177, passing close to the Fisheries Inn: a new housing development called 'Swan Reach' can be seen on the opposite bank of the canal and Pynesfield Lake is to the right. After Black Jack's Lock, which is set between a thatched cottage and Black Jack's Mill, leave the towpath and cross the canal using Bridge 178. Turn right at a T-junction of paths and, after about 100 yards, where the lane curves left, continue ahead, over a stile and along the footpath beyond, signposted as part of the Hillingdon Trail. The path goes uphill and half-left across a field and then between hedges, still ascending. Continue along a field edge and between two stiles, ignoring a footpath signposted to the right. Go over the stile at the top of the next field and then walk along a residential road. After 150 yards, turn left along a tarmac path and then go right at the corner of the school playground. This path brings you out at Harefield High Street: turn left to return to the crossroads and the green.

POINTS OF INTEREST:

Harefield – Harefield is perhaps best known for its hospital, but the village itself has something of a history. Buildings of note include St Mary's Church (a mile south of the main village), 17th-century cottages in the High Street and the Kings Arms Inn. The construction of the canal brought industry to the area and stimulated further residential development in the locality.

Stocker's Lake Nature Reserve – Situated at the northern end of the vast Colne Valley Park, the Reserve is noted for its birdlife, including Herons and Great Crested Grebes. The site is managed by the Hertfordshire and Middlesex Wildlife Trust.

REFRESHMENTS:

The Kings Arms, Harefield.
The Fisheries Inn, Coppermill Lock.

Walk 68   **JOYDEN'S WOOD**   5$\frac{1}{2}$m (8$\frac{3}{4}$km)

Maps: OS Sheets Landranger 177; Pathfinder 1176.

A walk from Old Bexley, discovering one of London's lesser known woodland areas.

Start: At 494735, Bexley Railway Station.

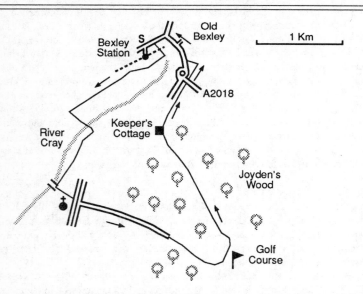

Leave the station and walk into Bexley High Street. Turn right down the High Street and then, almost immediately, right again down a small lane. Go under the railway bridge and follow the footpath past Bexley Cricket Club. Continue ahead, following the signs for 'Cray Riverway' and the yellow posts until you pass a pumping station. Here, go left along a footpath indicated by another Cray Riverway sign. Cross the river and turn right to continue along the waymarked riverside path to reach Five Arch Bridge. At the bridge turn left along a path, leaving the Cray Riverway. After about 100 yards this path forks: take the right-hand branch and continue ahead through St James's Churchyard.

Cross the dual carriageway, with great care, and continue along the minor road that can be seen opposite the church entrance. Go past a riding school and several houses and then, where the road bends sharply left, continue ahead along Parsonage Lane. The lane soon turns into an unmade track: continue along it, going gradually uphill to reach the entrance to **Joyden's Wood**.

Go over the stile ahead (to the left of a public footpath stone) and follow the path beyond to the edge of the wood, where there is a 'Beware of Golfers' sign. Now turn left at the double stile and follow a winding path just inside the wood, going along the edge of the golf course for about 400 yards.

As you leave the golf course, turn right, then immediately left along a major footpath towards the centre of the wood. Later, on your left, you may see a stone commemorating the opening of the wood in 1988: keep forward on the main path to eventually arrive at the Keeper's Cottage entrance. Go through the gates and follow the track to the right at the cottage. Go past Mount Mascal Farm and continue to reach the A2018 at Old Bexley. Cross the road, with care, and follow the footpath opposite, indicated by the 'Cray Riverway' sign. Shortly, at a T-junction of paths, turn left, to reach a road. At the road and St Mary's Church, go left, then right along Bexley High Street. Turn left at the roundabout and continue down the High Street to return to Bexley Station.

POINTS OF INTEREST:

Joyden's Wood – This Forestry Commission-owned wood is one of Greater London's best kept secrets. It has a wonderful atmosphere and provides very pleasant walking. A great variety of trees, flowers and wildlife can be found here, and all just 13 miles from the centre of the metropolis.

REFRESHMENTS:

The George, Bexley High Street.
There are many other possibilities close to the High Street.

Walk 69   COULSDON COMMON   5$\frac{1}{2}$m (8$\frac{3}{4}$km)

Maps: OS Sheets Landranger 187; Pathfinder 1207.
Farthing Downs and various Commons.
Start: At 300583, the car park on Farthing Downs.

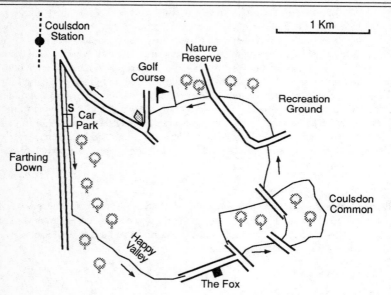

From the car park, head south (away from Coulsdon) over **Farthing Downs**, following the bridleway that runs parallel and to the left of the road. Go through a wooden gate and, after about 20 yards, turn left along a bridleway marked by blue posts, heading down towards the valley. Enter the woods, but do not go downhill along the bridleway: instead, turn right along a waymarked footpath, following it to the left of a wooden bench and seat made from trees split in half. Follow the path as it twists downhill through trees to reach a clearing. Continue to follow the path to 'Piles Wood 1$\frac{1}{4}$m'. The path, and the bridleway alongside it, cut a broad avenue through the trees. The path goes to the right of a group of trees and across a clearing in the lower part of the valley. There are two grass paths here and several crossing tracks, so take care: keep to the left-hand path and bear slightly left uphill to enter the trees where there are two sets of picnic benches. Now follow the signposted path to Coulsdon Common.

Avoid the footpath on the right to Ditches Lane, continuing to Coulsdon Common. The path turns into a tarmac drive and there is a fitness track nearby: at the car park, walk along the entrance road with the Fox Inn to your right. Cross the B2030, with care, and walk ahead along the tarmac path on to **Coulsdon Common**. After about 70 yards, bear right along a smaller path to reach Ninehams Road. This passes to the left of a cottage and enters the woods. Go past a pond and keep left on the main grass path which soon goes downhill to reach a road. Cross the road, but do not continue ahead, uphill: instead, bear left along the footpath signposted to Caterham Drive. Walk along Caterham Drive and, opposite Rydons Lane, turn right along the 'Bridle Road' to Hayes Lane. Climb steeply past a bungalow and then, after about 50 yards, take the prominent track on the left. The track bears left to the farm buildings, but you should continue ahead, going over a stile and walking alongside a fence, heading for the next stile and a footpath sign on Old Lodge Lane.

At the lane, turn right and walk past the Thatched Cottage to the Wattenden Arms. Just before the inn, turn left along the footpath to Hayes Lane. The path goes to the right of the fence: ignore a footpath to the right and continue forward towards Coulsdon. Now keep to the left of the recreation ground field. At the far end do not turn left: instead, walk ahead along a path marked by a yellow arrow. This path winds downhill through woods and brambles, eventually bringing you back to Old Lodge Lane.

Cross and continue along the signposted path into Dollypers Hill Reserve, avoiding the footpath that is not signposted. Continue ahead, crossing two tracks to reach a golf course. Walk straight across the golf course, route finding aided by the white marker posts. Go over a stile, cross Coulsdon Road and turn left. On reaching the Green, turn right along a gravel drive, going around a pond and then turning right into Marlpit Lane. Follow the Lane downhill past Coulsdon Memorial Ground and, opposite the Memorial Gardens, turn left to go uphill along Down Road. Go through the gate on to Farthing Downs and follow the bridleway back to the car park.

POINTS OF INTEREST:

Farthing Downs – In this chalk downland area Stone Age flint axes have ben found. Later, in the 7th century, the Saxons used part of the Downs as a burial ground. The area is now a Site of Special Scientific Interest.

Coulsdon Common – The Common is maintained by the Corporation of London and is protected from development by an 1878 Act of Parliament.

REFRESHMENTS:
The Fox, Fox Lane, Old Coulsdon.

Walk 70   **DOCKLANDS**   5$\frac{1}{2}$m (8$\frac{3}{4}$km)

Maps: OS Sheets Landranger 177; Pathfinder 1159 and 1175.

New and old dockland streets.

Start: At 374803, Canary Wharf, Docklands Light Railway Station.

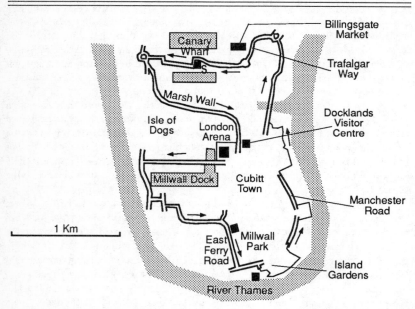

Leave the station by the Cabot Place West exit and walk across Cabot Square with its fountain. Look back for a close up view of **Canary Wharf**, one of London's most prominent skyline features. Continue along the left-hand side of West India Avenue and, at the roundabout, take the first path on the left. At the next roundabout, keep ahead and left along the road signposted to South Quay (Marsh Wall). Follow the road around, passing the International Hotel and the South Quay Plaza until Limeharbour appears on the right: go down here, following the elevated railway to reach the **Docklands Visitor Centre**. From the Visitor Centre, cross the road and follow the footpath indicated as a 'Dockside Walkway'. At the dockside, turn left to walk between the London Arena building and Millwall Inner Dock. At the end, turn right and cross Glengall Bridge. Continue along modern Pepper Street and, beyond the brick gateway, the more traditional Tiller Road. At the end, turn left along Westferry Road. Shortly after passing the Docklands Sailing Centre, turn left to enter the Timber Wharves Estate (Dockers Tanner Road). Turn right into Charnwood Gardens, following this residential road to its end where, as Copeland Drive, it forms a T-junction with Barnsdale Avenue. Turn right and then left at the next T-junction. Walk past Mudchute Station and keep ahead on East Ferry Road. Go over Chapel House Street and pass Millwall Park, on the left. At the crossroads, turn left along Manchester Road, turning right at Island Gardens Station. Walk past the entrance to the Greenwich Foot Tunnel to enter Island Gardens. Go through the gardens along the Thames-side path, continuing as the path passes to the right of several blocks of flats. At the Watermans Arms, turn right into Saunders Ness Road, a mainly residential street in Cubitt Town.

The route in this phase of the walk alternates between road and newly built sections of riverside path on the eastern side of the Isle of Dogs. At Sextant Avenue turn right: the two white obelisks at the end are in memory of six people who died in an explosion on this site in 1969. Turn left along the path by the river and left again at the end (into Chichester Way). Go down the steps and walk diagonally across Blyth Close to reach the main road (Manchester Road). Turn right and follow the road for about 300 yards to reach a sign for the Riverside Walkway. Now go right through the London Yard development, then left at the end to regain the river. After passing further blocks of flats the path turns away from the river once more: cross the road and walk to the right of Ballin Court, turning right again at the main road. Go over the bridge at the West India and Millwall Dock entrance and continue along Preston's Road to the roundabout next to Blackwall DLR Station. Now to complete the circuit, turn left along Trafalgar Way, following it for about $^1/_2$ mile to return to Canary Wharf.

POINTS OF INTEREST:
Canary Wharf – Now London's most prominent landmark, the official title for this 800 foot building is 'One Canada Square'. The tower houses a number of media offices. More skyscrapers are planned for the vicinity so perhaps one day Docklands will rival Manhattan!
Docklands Visitor Centre – The Centre houses an exhibition illustrating the regeneration of more than eight square miles of urban dockland area.

REFRESHMENTS:
There is a good cafeteria at the Cabot Square Shopping Centre.

Walks 71 & 72   GREEN CHAIN WALK   5¹/₂m (8³/₄km)
or 10¹/₂m (17km)

Maps: OS Sheets Landranger 177; Pathfinder 1176.
Woods, commons and parks.
Start: At 495792, Belvedere Railway Station.

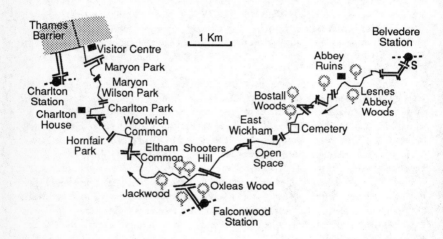

Walk past the tavern, cross Picardy Street and go to the right of the Belvedere, up
Picardy Road. Turn right along Upper Abbey Road at a sign to Lesnes Abbey. At the
end, go right, then left down Kingswood Avenue and immediately left again along a
drive. After 50 yards, bear left along a track, then right along a path marked by 'Green
Chain' posts. Follow the waymarkers through Lesnes Abbey Wood. At the bottom of
a hill, at a three-way sign, turn left for Bostall Wood. Cross a road and go through a
wood. At Hurst Lane, turn right and at the end go left for 30 yards. Cross and bear
right along a track to reach Bostall Hill Road. Turn right, cross at the sign and cross
Bostall Heath, keeping right of the trees. Cross a lane and join the path signed to East
Wickham. Go through Bostall Woods to join a drive by a cemetery. Go left along
Wickham Lane and right, uphill, after the Foresters Arms into East Wickham Open
Space. At the top, go past the signpost and, after about 200 yards, bear right along the

broad grass track to eventually reach a road. Go left, and then right along Dryden Road. Where this turns left, go ahead along the path to Oxleas Wood. Go through a gate and across a meadow. Towards the end, bear right through trees, and then left along the edge of another meadow. Cross a road and go right for about 60 yards. Turn left at the sign to enter Oxleas Wood. After about 300 yards the path joins a track going left and, after another 400 yards, the track reaches a three-way signpost.

The shorter walk goes ahead here. At the next post go left to reach a road junction. Go along Rochester Way for 500 yards to reach Falconwood Station. Trains run from here to Charing Cross and from there to the start at Belvedere.

The longer walk turns right towards Woolwich. Follow the waymarkers to a hill at Oxleas Meadow, then keep ahead towards Woolwich. Go around a plantation and turn left on meeting another broad drive. Go through the park and a wood. Go along a path and then right, up steps. At the top of the hill pass Severndroog Castle, then, just before a car park, go left to cross Eltham Common. Cross Shooters Hill and Academy Road at the lights, going right along the latter for 180 yards before bearing left at a sign, on to Woolwich Common. Fork left along a grass track near the Common's western edge. Walk along the road for 100 yards, then go right, next to a car park, through two gates into Hornfair Park. Follow signs along the Park's edge to reach Inigo Jones Road. Go right at the end, and then left into Canberra Road. After about 250 yards, turn right along a path across Charlton Park. After another 150 yards with Charlton House visible left, turn right and, at a car park, go left, then right along a road and left into Maryon Wilson Park. Follow the central path and, at the sign near the pens, turn right. Cross a road to enter Maryon Park. Go through a gate and half-right down steps. Turn left and pass two tennis courts, keeping forward at the Thames Barrier sign. After 100 yards, bear left to leave the park. Walk down a close to the main road and go left. Turn right along a footpath shortly before the Victoria Inn and keep ahead on an assortment of paths to reach the **Thames Barrier**. Go left through the tunnel and walk along the riverside for $^1/_2$ mile, turning left at Anchor and Hope Lane. Charlton Station, from where the start can be regained, is beyond the first set of traffic lights.

POINTS OF INTEREST:

Thames Barrier – Completed in 1984, the barrier has 9 piers and 10 steel flood gates, and is the official end point of the new Thames Path National Trail. There is a visitor centre and a cafe.

REFRESHMENTS:

There are possibilities at each end of the walk.

Walk 73   **FARNBOROUGH AND DOWNE**   5³/₄m (9¹/₂km)

Maps: OS Sheets Landranger 177; Pathfinder 1192.

A rural walk connecting two Kent villages.

Start: At 444641, St Giles Church, Farnborough village.

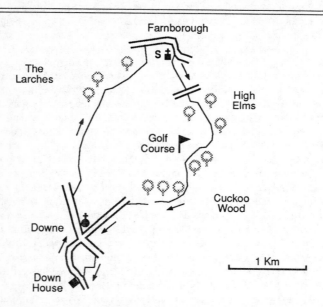

Leave the churchyard by the gate at the southern edge and follow the path straight ahead, signposted 'High Elms ¹/₄m', keeping the plantation to your left. Continue ahead into the plantation, cross a road and walk forward along a gravel path into **High Elms Country Park**. Go through the car park and turn right along a road at a sign for the High Elms Nature Centre. Follow the road around to the left, then continue ahead at a barrier, where the road turns into a gravel track. After about 200 yards, turn left along another gravel track to avoid the section of golf course directly ahead! At a crossing of paths, where there is a bench, turn right and follow the path around the northern edge of the golf course. At a track, with a clearing to your right, continue ahead along the smaller path. Soon, at a fork, take the left branch, go down some steps and then follow the path as it becomes gravel once more. Shortly, fork right, go through a gate and then go left along a path that keeps close to the edge of the golf course.

On meeting a fenced bridleway, turn left to follow the bridleway downhill. At the second path crossing, shortly before the fencing ends, turn right to continue through Cuckoo Wood. At the junction of paths, turn right and go uphill. Cross a stile and walk along the edge of the field beyond for about 100 yards, then follow the path as it veers left away from the wood, passing just to the right of the second pylon. Go over a stile and continue to a road. Turn left into Downe village, passing a recreation ground and a school. At the church turn left onto Cudham Road. Pass Christmas Tree Farm, then turn right on a track signposted for Luxted. At the back of the farm, cross a stile at a public footpath sign and turn right. Walk along the field edge, turning left at the corner to walk along the hedgerow. Leave the field at the next corner, going across the next field to emerge at **Down House**.

On leaving the house, turn left to follow the road back into Downe village. At the junction near the church, turn left to pass the Queen's Head, going along the High Street and Rookery Road. Ignore the first footpath sign to the right, passing 'Rookery Cottages' and 'The Orchard', to turn right at the next public footpath sign. Cross a stile and walk along the field edge to reach another stile, where there is a gap in the hedge. Follow the path to the left and cross the next field diagonally. Go through a gate, cross the farm track, and continue ahead along a footpath signposted 'Farnborough $1^1/_4$m'.

At a crossing of paths, continue forward, along a track, to the corner of a wood called 'The Larches'. Turn right at the road and go through a gap in the hedge, following the signposted path uphill, with the woods on your left. At the corner, enter the woods and follow the path to the right. The path leaves the wood and crosses a field, passing to the right of a small copse: continue forward, keeping to the edge of the field and then entering a tree-lined path. On reaching some steps, turn left and cross a playing field. Continue along a path that goes between houses to emerge into the residential part of Farnborough High Street. Turn right, then right again down Church Road to return to the start of the walk.

POINTS OF INTEREST:
High Elms Country Park – The Park has picnic areas and a number of nature trails. The Nature Centre has displays depicting the flora and fauna of the locality.
Down House – This property is the former residence of Charles Darwin, famous for his work on evolution. It is now the Darwin Museum.

REFRESHMENTS:
The George and Dragon, Downe.
The Woodman, Farnborough High Street.

Walk 74   HORNCHURCH   5³/₄m (9¹/₂km)

Maps: OS Sheets Landranger 177; Pathfinder 1160.
A country park in a suburban setting.
Start: At 539863, Hornchurch Underground Station.

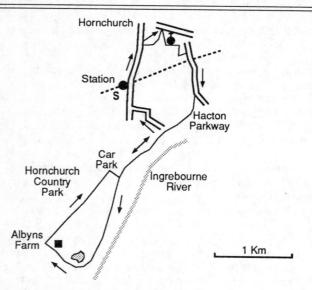

From the station forecourt, cross the road and turn left to head down Station Lane towards the centre of Hornchurch. Walk along this road for about ¹/₂ mile, then, almost opposite the Police Station and just before a parade of shops, take a footpath to the right, following it to a road. Cross and go through the small wooded area opposite to emerge at the car park for **St Andrew's Church**.

After visiting the church, leave by the gate where you entered, but turn immediately left along a tarmac drive, following it along the edge of the churchyard and bearing left through the cemetery. Now walk between the flats to reach a road. Turn left, cross the road, and at the junction with Hacton Lane turn right. Cross the railway bridge and continue along Bevan Way. Cross Central Drive and go straight ahead, along the pavement. Where the road bends sharply right, continue forward along a drive. This curves to the right and joins the Hacton Parkway alongside the Ingrebourne River.

The walk now begins to take on more of a rural character. Go through the wooden barriers marking the entrance to **Hornchurch Country Park** and follow the path beyond for about $1/_2$ mile to reach a picnic area with a car park nearby. Fork left along the smaller tarmac path, keeping the river to your left, then continue forward along the gravel path (this is the 'Eastern Pathway') signposted to Albyns Farm and Lake. Where this path forks, keep left. Shortly, the track goes up a small hill from where there are good views of the Country Park and back towards Hornchurch.

Continue down the hill and keep ahead, ignoring turnings to the right. The main track itself then curves right and left to pass between Albyns Lake and a fenced plantation. Continue along the gravel path to pass Albyns Farm. Shortly after the farm, go over a stile on the right (nearly opposite a small car park) and continue along the Western Pathway. Follow this well-defined grass pathway for about a mile, ignoring crossing tracks, to reach the corner of a residential area. The houses to your left were constructed on the former RAF Hornchurch Airfield.

Continue ahead, walking alongside the car park access road. At the car park, turn right and then left to return to the main tarmac path by the river (Hacton Parkway). Now follow this back to the entrance of of the Country Park. After going through the wooden entrance barriers, go left across the green to a T-junction of roads. Go forward, and then left up Ascot Gardens. Shortly after this bears right, turn left down Vaughan Avenue. Now turn right along Suttons Lane to return to Hornchurch Station.

POINTS OF INTEREST:

St Andrew's Church – The 120 foot high spire is a prominent landmark in the area. Over the East window there is a stone bull's head with a pair of horns – hence the name 'the Horned Church'. The bull is believed to represent the trade of tanning once popular in the locality.

Hornchurch Country Park – The Park has been developed predominantly on the site of RAF Hornchurch, famous as a Second World War fighter airfield. The RAF Station was closed in 1962 but many remains of the airfield can be seen from the walk. The park also includes Ingrebourne Marshes, a Site of Special Scientific Interest.

REFRESHMENTS:

The Railway Hotel, Station Lane, Hornchurch.
There are also a number of picnic sites in Hornchurch Country Park.

Walks 75 & 76   **GREAT WARLEY** $5^{3}/_{4}$m ($9^{1}/_{2}$km)
                                                 or 12m ($19^{1}/_{2}$km)

Maps: OS Sheets Landranger 177; Pathfinder 1141, 1142 and 1160.
A fine walk on country paths and bridleways.
Start: At 563906, the car park on Tyler's Common, on Nags
Head Lane between Upminster and Brentwood.

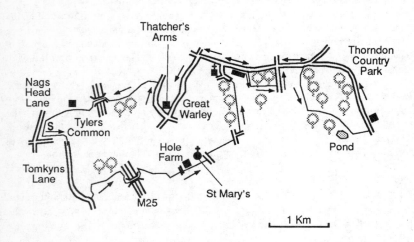

From the noticeboard in the corner of the car park, do not take the obvious track
uphill: instead, follow the smaller path between the picnic tables. After 400 yards,
bear half-left and head towards a telegraph pole. At the road, walk left, going along
the edge of the common to reach four posts. Now cross over and head down Tomkyns
Lane. Keep along this for $^{2}/_{3}$ mile. After the lane curves left, at the end of a group of
cottages, go left along a signposted path. Walk along the field edge, go over a stile
and along another field edge. After crossing the next stile, turn left along the uphill
permissive path. Turn right at the far corner (do not cross the stile). Go over a double
stile at the next corner and continue ahead to reach a fence close to the M25.

    Cross the footbridge over the M25 and turn left. From the electricity tower, walk
along the road for 40 yards and then turn sharp right over a stile. Go left around the

field. At the farm road turn right and, after passing Hole Farm, go left along the path to Warley Street. Turn left at the road to visit **St Mary the Virgin** Church. From the gate, cross the road, go over a stile and along the footpath beyond. Climb the next stile and cross the field beyond, aiming for a small post. Cross a bridge and a stile and continue over the hill. Go through two farm gates to reach Bird Lane. Go left, and then right down Magpie Lane. Turn left at the footpath sign at the next junction and follow the path for $^2/_3$ mile to Warley Gap. At the road, turn left, and then right, passing the Regimental Chapel to reach a T-junction. The shorter walk turns left here.

The longer walk turns right, passing the Ford buildings. At the end of the fence, turn right along a footpath. Go through an avenue of trees and along a field edge to reach a tennis club. Turn left and walk along the lane to reach a crossroads. Turn right to reach the entrance to **Thorndon Country Park**. Go through the Lion Gate and, after 20 yards, turn right along the 'Horseride'. Follow the bridleway for a mile to reach a T-junction of paths. Here the horseride goes left, but you should go right, along the footpath. Go past a pond and then follow the path leftwards and uphill. When you reach a triangular clearing near the top of the hill, bear right along a path indicated by a red arrow. This path emerges from the woods at a pond. After the 'No Fishing' notice, turn left and go through a gap in the fence. Cross the small bridge on the left and follow the path uphill along the field edge. At the top of the hill there is a meeting of paths close to Hatch Farm: go left along the farm track, following it for a mile, passing two car parks. Go through the Lion Gate and left along the road for nearly a mile, joining the shorter walk before reaching the Horse and Groom.

Turn left and follow the path by the road for $^1/_2$ mile to reach the Thatchers Arms. Go right down Dark Lane (behind the inn), and, after the second set of cottages, cross the stile on the left to join a path to Tylers Common. Go over another stile and veer left, uphill, from the corner of a field. Go over the next stile, along the edge of a large field and through a wood. Continue along the permissive path to the M25 bridge. Cross the bridge, turn left and then go right at a stile. At the next stile a sign indicates the direction across Tyler's Common back to the starting car park.

POINTS OF INTEREST:

St Mary the Virgin – The church has an attractive exterior and an art nouveau interior.
Thorndon Country Park – The Park's Visitor Centre was constructed from trees blown down in the hurricane of 1987.

REFRESHMENTS:

The Horse and Groom, Great Warley.
The Thatcher's Arms, Great Warley.

Walk 77   **CHALDON CIRCUIT**   5³/₄m (9¹/₂km)

Maps: OS Sheets Landranger 187; Pathfinder 1207.

A downland circuit of Chaldon village, using a section of the North Downs Way.

Start: At 317568, the Fox Lane car park, Coulsdon Common.

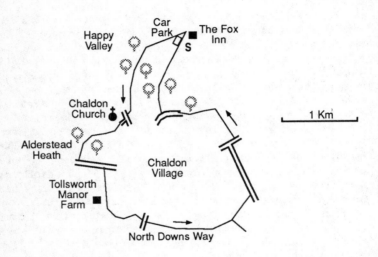

From the car park, head westwards past an information board, following the tarmac walkway signposted as the 'Downlands Circular Walk', the first part of this route coinciding with this waymarked walk. Soon the tarmac ends and the path descends into the trees: after about 60 yards, turn left along another footpath, signposted to Ditches Lane, going steeply downhill initially. Cross another track in **Happy Valley** and then keep ahead, uphill, with a hedgerow to your left. Continue into the trees and then walk across a large farm field. Now go left along Ditches Lane for about 40 yards, and then bear right along the tarmac drive passing **Chaldon Church**. Shortly beyond the church, leave the drive, going left over a stile on to a footpath to Alderstead Heath. Cross a field and, at the next stile, bear right along the field edge, as waymarked. After about 300 yards the path goes left, cutting across the corner of the field. Go over a stile to reach a corner of Furzefield Wood. Go over another stile into the wood and turn left along a concrete driveway, ignoring another concrete drive ahead. At a T-junction, go left along a path to reach Dean Lane. Go left, following the path by the hedge beside the lane. After approximately 300 yards, cross the road and walk along the drive (signposted as a bridleway) to Tollsworth Manor Farm. Pass Tollsworth Cottages and the 15th-century farmhouse, go left, briefly, and then right, following the bridleway by the edge of the field and ignoring a footpath signposted to the right. At the top of the field there are good views north and south and some of London's tallest buildings are visible on clear days. The bridleway goes through a gate and curves left to join the North Downs Way. Stay on the North Downs Way now for about a mile, following the acorn symbols.

The track along the Downs crosses Hilltop Lane and passes Hilltop Farm. After a further $^1/_2$ mile, ignore the Downlands Circular Walk sign indicating a path to the left, continuing along the North Downs Way. Shortly after passing Willey Park Farm, at a fenced pond, the Way curves right, but our walk continues forward on another tarmac drive, heading downhill to Roffes Lane. At the lane, turn immediately left to walk along Chaldon Common Road. At the end of this, cross and walk right along Rook Lane. After 30 yards, turn left over a stile into a field. Walk along the grass path close to the right-hand edge of the field, crossing a small ditch and entering another field. About 80 yards into this field, turn left along another grass path. This path passes between two trees and crosses a small meadow. At the next field corner, follow the path downhill and then half-right diagonally across the field. At the end of the field, fork left along a path going slightly uphill to reach some trees, a gate and a residential road. Walk forward along the road for about 300 yards to the point where it turns sharply left. Here, turn right along a gravel bridleway, following it for over $^1/_2$ mile, passing between Piles Wood and Broad Wood. Pass a stile on the left and then keep ahead at a crossing of paths, heading in the direction of '$^1/_4$m Coulsdon Common'. Ignore a right fork and then, when you meet a path crossroads, keep ahead into a small dip through the trees. Cross the next two fields to return the car park.

POINTS OF INTEREST:
Happy Valley – The valley and its surrounding woods and commons provide a very pleasant area for ramblers and nature watchers.
Chaldon Church – The Church of St Peter and St Paul, in its charming rural location, is about 1000 years old and has a rare wall painting on its west wall.

REFRESHMENTS:
The Fox, Fox Lane, Old Coulsdon, close to the start of the walk.

Walk 78   **HAVERING AND HAINAULT FOREST**   6m (9$\frac{1}{2}$km)
Maps: OS Sheets Landranger 177; Pathfinder 1141.
A moderate walk between two Country Parks, mainly on woodland footpaths and bridleways.
Start: At 512931, St John's Church, Havering-atte-Bower.

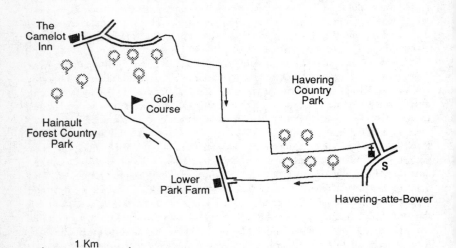

Walk along the path on the green in front of the church and turn right down Orange Tree Hill. After passing The Orange Tree Inn, turn right down Pinewood Road. Pass a number of gardens and a barn to enter the woods of **Havering Country Park**. Keep on the track ahead, passing the Park Office and an information board. Further on, go past a car park on your left and at the crossing beyond continue ahead along a bridleway, going away from the woods and towards a farm. On reaching an unmade road, continue ahead maintaining an easterly direction.

Go across a stream and continue to reach Lower Park Farm. Follow the road around to the right and, about 100 yards after the farm, go over a stile on the left and follow a footpath along the field edge. At a gap in the hedgerow, where there is a footpath post with a yellow arrow, turn right along another field edge path. Go through another gap in the hedgerow, at a sign indicating 'Footpath No.1 Hainault Forest', and cross the field beyond to reach a stile. Go over to reach the edge of a golf course.

Carefully follow the yellow marker posts across the golf course fairways to reach a gate and a stile close to the summit of Cabin Hill. Go over the stile and turn right along a track. At the **Hainault Forest Country Park** information point and map board, turn right along a well-defined path. Follow this path through the forest, ignoring paths to the left and right, going steadily downhill to eventually arrive at a car park and the Camelot Inn.

At the inn, turn right and follow the road for about 100 yards, re-entering the Country Park via the drive on the right, before a bungalow. Follow the drive along the northern edge of the forest, passing the buildings of Crabtree Hill. Shortly, at a T-junction of footpaths, turn left, passing an old London County Council boundary post. Do not cross the stile: instead, follow the path round to the right. There are good views of Havering from this point. At a marker post, turn left to head away from Hainault Forest along a link path back to Havering Country Park. The path turns right to cross a stream and then goes left at the corner of a small wood. Walk uphill towards Bower Farm, but before reaching it turn right along a bridleway. Walk uphill past the Havering Country Park sign and then take the next track left, where there are three wooden posts. At a major crossing continue straight ahead, passing riding stables before returning to St John's Church, Havering-atte-Bower.

POINTS OF INTEREST:

Havering Country Park – The Park covers over 100 acres of surprisingly unspoilt and varied woodland habitats despite its close proximity to built-up areas.

Hainault Forest Country Park – The Park provides a very popular recreation area for the people of East London and Essex at weekends. Activities include golf, fishing, horse riding and mountain biking. The walk goes through one of the older sections of this former royal hunting forest. The different habitat types in the area support a variety of birds.

REFRESHMENTS:

The Orange Tree, Havering-atte-Bower.
The Camelot, Lambourne End near Chigwell Row.

Walk 79   **BIGGIN HILL** $6^1/_4$m (10km)

Maps: OS Sheets Landranger 187; Pathfinder 1192 and 1208.
A circuit on roads and undulating footpaths.
Start: At 414619, Leaves Green Common car park.

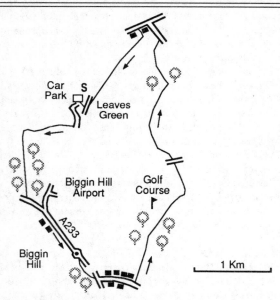

This is a circular route around Biggin Hill airfield and along the eastern side of West Kent Golf Club. The first half of the walk includes some roads, but the later sections are almost entirely on country paths.

From the car park entrance at **Leaves Green Common**, cross Ashmore Lane and keep ahead to follow the tarmac drive (Leaves Green Crescent) past a row of stone-clad cottages and along the western edge of the Common. Walk on the pavement for a few yards, then, opposite Milking Lane and the Kings Arms, turn right along a public byway, following it as it joins a tarmac drive and passes High House Farm. Shortly, cross a stile to the left of the gate to Ashmore Farm and follow the path beyond to another farm drive. After about 100 yards, cross the stile indicated by yellow arrows and head left. Cross another stile, turn left and follow the field's edge

154

admiring the views into the valley below. Cross a stile by a gate and follow the path beyond through the woods, ignoring a path to the left to reach a road.

Turn left and walk up Saltbox Hill for about 400 yards. At the main road, turn right towards Biggin Hill. Follow the road for about $^1/_3$ mile, with **Biggin Hill Airport** on the left, to pass a roundabout. About 300 yards after the roundabout, go right down a set of wooden steps and along a footpath. Go past various pieces of keep fit equipment, then fork left back to the main road. Cross, with care, and walk down Jail Lane for about $^1/_3$ mile, then turn left along a signed footpath. This path povides a pleasant change to the roads, taking the walker along the bottom of a dip and into Snotsdale Wood. Go through a metal kissing gate to enter the woods and then keep ahead, ignoring a left fork. The track soon leaves the wood and goes across the West Kent Golf Course, guided by a line of silver birch trees. After passing the last of the trees, head uphill and go through the gap in the hedge. Turn left along a footpath, following it for $1^1/_4$ miles to reach Holwood Farm.

After a short distance, cross a minor road and keep ahead to reach a T-junction of paths. Turn left (signposted Cudham Circular Walk) and go through a wooded area. Go over a stile on to a hill, with the golf course and clubhouse to the left. Go over two more stiles, across a field and through a kissing gate into a wood. Leave the wood through a similar gate with a 'Leaves Green Circular Walk' marker. Go over the stile at the far side of the next field and follow the path left. When crossing the next field, take care to keep to the left-hand side, with the trees to your left, until you see a yellow marker post ahead. The route now passes under the electricity lines to reach a road. Turn left, passing the Keston sign, and keep left where the road bends. Shortly, turn left along a tarmac footpath to Leaves Green. This path crosses a large field to reach a crossing with a farm track: keep ahead, going diagonally along a narrow footpath across another big field. At the end, go over a stile and turn right to walk across a section of the Common to return to the car park.

POINTS OF INTEREST:

Leaves Green Common – A noticeboard provides details of a circular walk connecting a number of nearby villages.

Biggin Hill Airport – The Hurricane and Spitfire aircraft near the airfield entrance testify to the site's importance during the Second World War, particularly as a Battle of Britain base. Nowadays it is used by small commercial and recreational aircraft.

REFRESHMENTS:

The Kings Arms, Leaves Green.

There is a cafeteria near the entrance to Biggin Hill Airport.

Walk 80   HENDON CIRCUIT   6¹/₄m (10km)

Maps: OS Sheets Landranger 176; Pathfinder 1140 and 1159.
A circular tour of Hendon parks.
Start: At 230886, Hendon Central Underground Station.

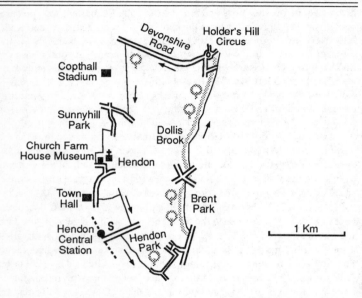

From the station exit, turn left along Queen's Road. After about 200 yards, cross and
enter Hendon Park. Walk along the path between the 'Quiet Garden' and the tennis
courts and, at the end of the play area, go right and then left along a smaller path.
Follow this path along the edge of the park to reach a road. Cross and walk along
another road (Shirehall Park). After about 100 yards, stay on Shirehall Park as it
branches off to the left. Walk past bungalows and, after about 500 yards, stay on the
road as it turns sharply left. About 40 yards after this, go right at a link road. At a
T-junction, cross and walk right along Brent Street to reach the lights. Now follow
the pavement leftwards, alongside the North Circular Road, passing Brook Lodge.
Soon there are green railings and a gate on your left: go through the gate and follow
the surfaced path beside Dollis Brook. Follow the path through Brent Park, with the
brook and a lake to your left. At the end of the lake, go through a gate and turn left

156

along Bridge Lane. At the bridge, cross and continue along Brookside Walk. This section of path is part of the Dollis Valley Greenwalk and stays close to the brook, soon passing under two road bridges. The route now crosses Waverley Grove and enters Windsor Open Space. Continue to follow the Dollis Valley Greenwalk signs until they direct you over the brook at a footbridge. After crossing the bridge, turn immediately left to walk down a tree-lined cul-de-sac. At the end, turn right and at the roundabout cross and go past the Mill Inn to walk along Devonshire Road. After $^1/_2$ mile, at a bridge, go left down the steps and follow a tarmac path beside the disused railway for a short distance. Go past a metal gate and then, about 20 yards further on, at a wooden gate, turn left along a gravel path. Cross a car parking area and walk between allotments to reach a minor road next to the busy A1.

Turn right and walk beside the A1 to reach a footbridge. Cross and continue along Sunny Gardens Road. After about 250 yards, turn right into **Sunny Hill Park**. Once inside the Park, take the first path on the left, following the Park's eastern edge, admiring the views westwards as you climb the hill. At the crossing of paths just beyond the summit, turn left. Now, at the far corner (at a small building) do not leave the Park: instead, turn right and walk downhill on the grass to reach another surfaced path. Turn left along this, walking uphill to reach Greyhound Hill. Turn left and walk past **Church Farmhouse Museum** and St Mary's Church. Follow the road around to the right and, at the junction with Church Road, turn right to walk past the Middlesex University buildings and Hendon Library. Cross at the lights close to the Town Hall and continue towards the Methodist Church. Immediately before the church, turn left along the Chapel Walk footpath. Where this forms a T-junction, turn right into another alleyway (West View). Stay on this path until it ends at a road opposite Hendon Park. Now turn right to return to Hendon Central Station.

POINTS OF INTEREST:

Sunny Hill Park – From the summit of the hill in this pleasant open space there are good views across North London and beyond. The Hendon RAF Museum can be seen in the near distance, on the other side of the M1, and Wembley Stadium may also be visible.

Church Farmhouse Museum – The house, built around 1660, is one of the oldest surviving dwellings in the Borough of Barnet. It now contains a charming museum with an 1820s kitchen and an 1850s dining room, along with a variety of exhibits.

REFRESHMENTS:

The Mill Inn, Holder's Hill Circus.
The Greyhound Inn, Greyhound Hill, Hendon.

Walk 81   WIMBLEDON COMMON   6¼m (10km)

Maps: OS Sheets Landranger 176; Pathfinder 1175.

Exploring the open spaces and woods of Wimbledon Common and Putney Heath. Can be muddy in winter.

Start: At 248707, Wimbledon Station (Rail and Underground).

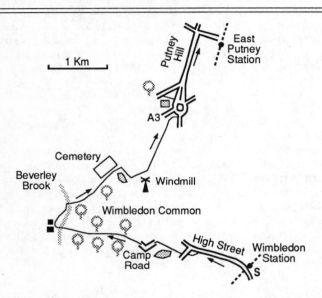

From the station turn right up Wimbledon Hill Road towards Wimbledon Village. At the first mini-roundabout, turn right, and at the second go left. Where the High Street bears left, you should go left too: **Wimbledon Common** is now to your right. Turn right down The Green and, almost immediately, bear left along the diagonal gravel path, keeping a pond to your left. Cross a road and continue along the gravel path to reach a crossroads where Wimbledon seems to retain its 'village' atmosphere. Turn left down Camp Road and walk past the Fox and Grapes Inn.

At Wimbledon Common Golf Club, go forward along the middle of the three roads, the one with signs indicating 'Authorised Vehicles Only'. Go past a white bungalow and a white gate, continuing along this well-defined track through woodland for about ³⁄₄ mile to reach a small brick bridge on the western edge of the Common.

Cross the bridge and turn immediately right to follow a small footpath adjacent to the stream. Continue to the point where the path goes along the edge of a playing field and then cross the brook by means of a footbridge.

From the far side of the footbridge walk straight ahead along the edge of another playing field. Just after the War Memorial the path re-enters the woods: turn left along the uphill track to maintain direction along the northern edge of the woods, with Putney Vale Cemetery shortly appearing on your left. Before reaching the eastern end of the cemetery, turn right along a smaller footpath (opposite the cemetery gate). Now walk along the edge of Queen's Mere, and from its south-eastern end take the left-hand path of the three, going uphill to a car park, the London Scottish Golf Clubhouse and the rather surprising sight of a windmill! Walk across the car park and turn right to pass **Wimbledon Windmill Museum** and the rear of the windmill itself. At the crossroads, turn left along a track. In about 100 yards, after a cattle trough, this forks three ways: take the centre track and follow it (or the parallel track a few yards to the left) across **Putney Heath** for about $^3/_4$ mile to reach the A3 roundabout. Go under the roundabout, using one of the pedestrian subways, to emerge in Kingston Road North: a large traffic sign indicates that this point is just 6 miles from the West End. Follow the footpath by the road for about 50 yards, then turn left along a small footpath, with a reservoir fence to your left. At the end of the path, turn right along a road which will take you to the corner of Putney Heath and a set of traffic lights. From here (opposite 'The Green Man') there are frequent buses into Putney.

Those wishing to finish the excursion on foot should continue down Putney Hill to the next major set of traffic lights (for Putney Rail Station) and turn right there along the South Circular Road, shortly reaching East Putney Underground Station from where there are frequent District Line trains to Wimbledon.

POINTS OF INTEREST:

Wimbledon Common - The Common provides 1,100 acres of recreational area for Londoners. It is easily accessed and includes heath, woodland and scrub.
Wimbledon Windmill Museum - Located at the centre of Wimbledon Common, the restored windmill and the museum are well worth a visit. There is also a tea room.
Putney Heath - Putney Heath was once famous as a site of duels and is also alleged to have been a haunt of highwaymen.

REFRESHMENTS:

The Fox and Grapes, Camp Road, Wimbledon.
There are many other inns and restaurants in Wimbledon and Putney also offers a whole range of choices.

Walk 82   **FRYENT COUNTRY PARK**   6¼m (10km)

Maps: OS Sheets Landranger 176; Pathfinder 1158 and 1159.
A circuit of North London parks.
Start: At 194863, Wembley Park Underground Station.

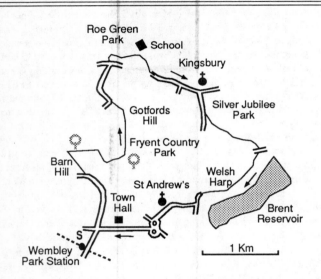

Turn left from the station to walk along Bridge Road. At the traffic lights continue
ahead up Barn Hill. After about ½ mile, where the road turns sharply left, you will
reach Barn Hill Open Space, part of **Fryent Country Park**. Walk half-right past a
barrier and then go along a path between the trees. After about 80 yards, fork left
along another path, following it to a fish pond. A triangulation point marks the summit
of the hill and there is a good view towards Wembley Stadium. Walk around the
pond to its north-western bank from where there are two paths heading downhill:
take the prominent left-hand track which goes into the trees, ignoring another, smaller,
footpath going left. Follow the track downhill until, a few yards before it enters a
large open field, it meets a crossing path just inside the woods. Turn sharp right here
and walk along the path inside the northern and the eastern edges of the woods until a
car park can be seen to the left. Walk through the car park, go under the barrier and
cross the road to enter another section of the Country Park.

From the small parking area, follow the grass path that heads to the right of a group of trees. Keep on this for a further 200 yards until an obvious gap in the hedgerow and a path appear on the left. Now take this grass path towards the summit of Gotfords Hill. Follow the path through two more hedges and over the hilltop, admiring the view westwards towards Harrow. Continue down the hill and pass a gate to reach a road. Turn right and follow the road to reach a main road. Cross, with care, and go slightly left to join a drive into Roe Green Park. Where this drive forks, keep right to walk past the Veterans Club. As you approach a school, turn sharp right along another tarmac path, and where this forks bear left. At the next path junction, turn right to head for the south-east corner of the park. Now walk along the main Kingsbury Road for nearly $\frac{1}{2}$ mile.

Just before Kingsbury Church, cross and go right along the footpath between Townsend Lane and Silver Jubilee Park. Go past a play area, then leave the path, bearing half-left, diagonally crossing the playing field. Go up a bank next to an oak tree and maintain direction across the next field, heading for a group of trees on a small hill. At the corner, go right up a grass track with a wire fence to your left. After 50 yards, fork left along a smaller path, keeping left to reach a road. Cross, go left for about 30 yards, and then turn right into Woodfield Park. Go diagonally across the playing field, with the sailing club to your left, to reach, about 20 yards right of the corner of the Park, two planks over a stream. Cross and, after a few yards, bear left along a small grass path. Turn right along the main path close to **Brent Reservoir**: this turns to tarmac as it crosses the Welsh Harp open space. Continue along the road, following it leftwards for about 150 yards before turning right along a lane next to a green. At the lych-gate, turn right into the churchyard. Walk past old St Andrew's Church and, at a gate, turn left to pass the more recent version. Leave by the left-hand gate and walk along the right side of Tudor Gardens. Cross Salmon Street at the first roundabout. Use the pedestrian crossing and turn right to walk along Forty Lane, passing Brent Town Hall. At Bridge Street turn left to return to Wembley Park Station.

POINTS OF INTEREST:
Fryent Country Park - This extensive Park is a 'regional open space'. It includes Barn Hill, which was originally landscaped by Repton, and Gotfords Hill.
Brent Reservoir - The reservoir is one of London's most popular sites for ornithologists. The waters are also used by windsurfers and sailing boats.

REFRESHMENTS:
There are possibilities at Wembley Park and Kingsbury.

Walk 83　　　EPPING FOREST　　　6½m (10½km)

Maps: OS Sheets Landranger 177; Pathfinder 1141.

An exploration of the old hunting forest.

Start: At 398947, the car park for the Queen Elizabeth Hunting Lodge.

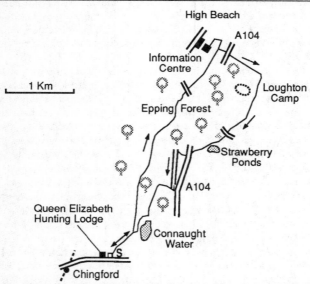

From the car park cross the road to visit the **Queen Elizabeth Hunting Lodge**, now the Epping Forest Museum. From the Lodge, walk along the road, passing the Butler's Retreat restaurant, and turn left along a bridleway marked by white posts. Follow the posts, walking ahead to enter the forest along a wide, well-defined track. In total the Forest covers an area of 6,000 acres and is approximately 12 miles long. Follow the track for approximately ¾ mile to reach an obvious fork. Take the left-hand branch, going slightly uphill along the gravel track to reach a partly-open area called Whitehouse Plain, where the track veers left back into the trees. This section of the route is part of the Forest Centenary Walk devised by Fred Matthews and Harry Bittern. It twists and turns, and climbs steadily uphill to reach the High Beach to Loughton road. Cross the road and continue along the well-defined gravel track opposite. Follow this track for just over $^1/_2$ mile until you reach its crossroads with a gravel path for the disabled. Turn left along this path, and then left again to visit the **Epping Forest Information Centre**. The Kings Oak Inn is on the road beyond the centre.

To continue the walk, go back along the wheelchair path to the crossing and turn right. Retrace your steps for about another 300 yards and then, at the small triangular green, turn left. Shortly, cross the A104, with care, and follow the track opposite, passing to the right of a small car park. Follow the path south-eastwards for about $^1/_2$ mile through what might be described as the 'heart' of the forest. Ignore a left turn, but immediately after this turn right along a well-defined, sandy track. The Iron Age Loughton Camp earthworks are soon to your right. Follow the path downhill and over Loughton Brook. This section of the route follows the Three Forests Way which connects Epping, Hainault and Hatfield Forests.

Cross a road and take the path opposite along the left-hand side of a pond. After about 200 yards, take a right fork to walk along the northern edge of the second of Strawberry Hill's ponds. The path crosses a small open area and then re-enters the woods, soon reaching a small car park and the A104. Cross the road, with care, and proceed half-right along the gravel footpath, not the grass bridleway. At the point where this footpath reaches a minor road, turn left along the bridleway running beside the road. After nearly $^1/_2$ mile the bridleway crosses the road and enters an area of forest called 'The Warren'. Continue along the track to reach a T-junction. Keep left, and at the next crossing of paths turn left again. After 400 yards the path reaches the bridleway that was followed during the first part of the walk: reverse the outward route uphill back to the Queen Elizabeth Hunting Lodge.

POINTS OF INTEREST:

The Queen Elizabeth Hunting Lodge - This listed building, not far from Chingford Station, is a unique example of a timber-framed Tudor Hunt standing. The upper floors were open so that hunting could be carried out from within the building! The lodge was extensively repaired and renovated in 1992/3 and now houses the Epping Forest Museum.

Epping Forest Information Centre - Although only a relatively small building, this Information Centre, opened in 1993, contains a wealth of useful information on the forest's natural history and recreational uses.

REFRESHMENTS:

The Butler's Retreat, near the start of the walk.
The King's Oak, High Beach.

Walks 84 & 85 RICHMOND PARK 6½m (10½km) or 8m (12¾km)

Maps: OS Sheets Landranger 176; Pathfinder 1174 and 1175.
A circular walk around London's Largest Royal Park.
Start: At 181752, Richmond Station (Rail and Underground).

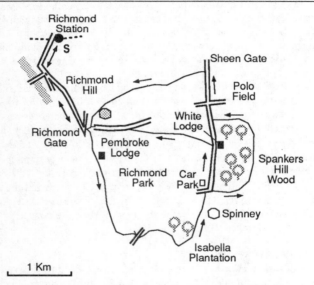

From the station, turn left along Richmond's main shopping street, following it into the town centre and left towards Richmond Bridge. At the mini-roundabout, go ahead, then left up Hill Rise (not along the A307 main road). Hill Rise soon becomes Richmond Hill: continue along it, passing the Star and Garter Home. Cross the road and enter Richmond Park at Richmond Gate. Immediately turn right along a tarmac footpath, following it to reach the black iron gate into Pembroke Lodge Gardens. Go through, and along Laburnum Walk to emerge near the **Henry VIII Mound**. Now keep to the right-hand side of the formal gardens and then to the right of Pembroke Lodge. Follow the path until it bends sharply left to begin its return towards Pembroke Lodge. Here, go ahead along a smaller path and leave the gardens through a gate. Head southwards along Hornbeam Walk and, at the point where the path goes close to a road, bear slightly right along a grass track through bracken. At a large tree stump, turn half-left along another grass track leading back to the road. Cross the road near the crossroads and follow the sign, left, for 'Isabella: Invalid Car Park Only'. After about 50 yards bear half-right along a grass path (a short cut to the car park). Go through the gate into the **Isabella Plantation** and walk to the right of Peg's Pond. Follow the gravel path to the right of the main stream through the plantation. Do not cross any of the small wooden bridges except the one over a tributary of the stream. After about 400 yards you will reach an iron fence marking the eastern boundary of the plantation: turn left, cross the bridge and leave through a gate. Now do not follow the main track to the Broomfield Hill car park: instead, take the middle of the three grass tracks going uphill to the left, following it to the left of Prince Charles's Spinney. From the corner of the spinney go towards the car park, reaching a road just before it. Turn right to reach a T-junction.

The shorter walk turns left and follows the road to White Lodge. Ignore a path to the right and, when you are level with the main building, turn left to walk along The Queen's Drive, following it for about a mile to reach Sawyer's Hill. Follow the road to reach Richmond Gate and the longer walk.

At the T-junction, the longer walk ignores all roads, going ahead, uphill, along a grass path that goes to the right of Spankers Hill Wood. Follow the edge of the wood and then go downhill between groups of trees. At a junction of paths near a wooden fence, turn right and walk with the fence on your left to reach the next fence corner. Now continue ahead for about 200 yards, then bear half-left on a path along the edge of a wooded section, with 'The Polo Field' to your right. Follow the path to a road and turn right. Go straight over at a crossroads, continuing to reach Sheen Gate. Just before the Sheen Gate car park, turn left along a footpath, following it around the northern perimeter of the park to reach Richmond Gate, passing three other Gates and Bishop's Pond en route.

From Richmond Gate, reverse the outward route back to the start.

POINTS OF INTEREST:
Henry VIII Mound - The mound may have been a Bronze Age Barrow and is the highest point in Richmond Park.
Isabella Plantation - Along with the Pen Ponds this is probably one of the most popular areas within Richmond Park.

REFRESHMENTS:
The Roebuck, Richmond Hill.
Pembroke Lodge, Richmond Park.

Walk 86   CHISLEHURST AND PETTS WOOD   6½m (10½km)

Maps: OS Sheets Landranger 177; Pathfinder 1176 and 1192.

Country commons and woods.

Start: At 444699, Chislehurst Parish Church, on the B264.

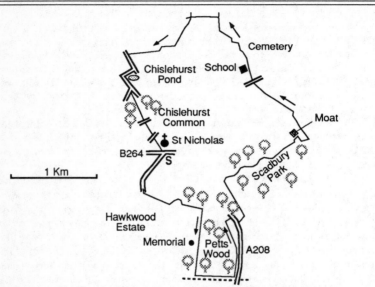

From the lych-gate of St Nicholas's Church, cross the B264, with care, and go down Hawkwood Lane, which bears left as a bridleway at Hawk's Wing. After about 200 yards, turn left along a public footpath.

Follow the path as it passes between a school field and the Hawkwood Estate. The path curves right into a wood, goes left around a pond and then goes right uphill. When you reach a crossing of paths near the crest of the hill, do not turn left into the woods: instead, continue ahead along the field edge. After about 200 yards you will meet a crossing track just inside the wood: turn right along this into **Petts Wood**. After ¼ mile, a memorial stone can be seen in a clearing to the right: continue ahead for another ¼ mile to reach the corner of the wood. A railway can be seen ahead: turn left and walk along the southern edge of the wood, keeping the railway to your right.

When a house and a road come into sight ahead you have reached the south-eastern corner of the wood: stay with the bridleway as it curves left and then runs parallel with the road. Ignore all crossing paths to reach, after $^1/_3$ mile, a barrier between two trees. Fork left here and walk between the blue and white marked trees. After $^1/_4$ mile, next to a large oak tree with a fallen tree behind it, there is a crossing of paths: leave the bridleway here, turning right to reach a road. Cross the road, turn right and follow the gravel path beside the road for roughly 100 yards. About 20 yards before the Give Way sign, turn left along a path. At the first crossing of paths, turn left. Walk forward across a bridleway at the barriers and keep on the well-defined path for $^1/_4$ mile until a public footpath appears on the right.

Now walk between the wooden posts along this path, almost immediately bearing left into **Scadbury Park**. After a few yards, bear right and then right again to go along the main path through the reserve. After nearly $^1/_2$ mile, detour left to visit the moated site of Scadbury Manor. Return to the main path, bearing left at a bench and going left, uphill, at the next T-junction. At the crossing, go through the gate and continue along the track in the field. Go down steps and then uphill towards a house. Pass the house at a gate and then go through another gate to reach a road. Turn right and walk to the Perry Street exit. Cross over and walk along Beaverwood Road, then keep ahead along the footpath to Chislehurst reached to the left of the cemetery gates. Bear left at the end of the cemetery fence and, shortly, go over a stile and walk towards a gate on the other side of a field. Do not go through the gate: instead, turn right to walk along the edge of the field. At the corner, go over the left-hand stile. At the end of the railed fence the path joins a track: turn left and walk downhill, turning left again along a gravel lane at the next junction.

After the first house on the right, turn along a tarmac path. At the end, turn left and walk along Green Lane until Chislehurst Pond appears. Now cross and follow the path beside the pond. Cross the High Street and turn left. Cross Imperial Prince Road and join the footpath on to Chislehurst Common at the white stone posts. Ignore the right and left forks, continuing along the main path to reach a road. Cross and maintain direction along another footpath. At the school, cross the next road and walk over the final section of Common to reach the church.

POINTS OF INTEREST:

Petts Wood - This fine, 88 acre wood is now a National Trust property.
Scadbury Park - The Park includes a nature trail and the remains of a moated manor house.

REFRESHMENTS:

The Queen's Head, Chislehurst Pond.

Walk 87   **THE RIVER LEA** $6\frac{1}{2}$m ($10\frac{1}{2}$km)

Maps: OS Sheets Landranger 177; Pathfinder 1159.

River, canal, parks and nature reserves.

Start: At 345895, Tottenham Hale Rail and Underground Station.

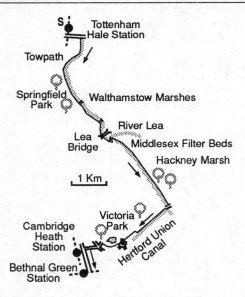

The route follows the course of the River Lea for about 4 miles and then heads west through Victoria Park to finish either at Cambridge Heath Rail Station or Bethnal Green Underground Station.

From Tottenham Hale Station use the pedestrian subway to Ferry Lane South. From the subway exit, turn right along Ferry Lane, immediately crossing the railway. After about 300 yards, at a road bridge over the River Lea, turn right and walk down the ramp to join the towpath. Follow the towpath past the Narrow Boat Inn and a modern housing development. About a mile further on the path passes the Lea Rowing Club and runs alongside Springfield Park: use the footbridge next to the tennis courts to cross the river and turn right to continue southwards along the river close to **Walthamstow Marsh Nature Reserve**. Go under the A V Roe Arches (carrying the railway) and, just before the Lea Valley Ice Rink, cross another footbridge over the river. Go around a bend in the river and pass under Lea Bridge Road. Shortly after passing the Prince of Wales Inn and Lea Bridge Weir, cross another footbridge to pass the **Middlesex Filter Beds Nature Reserve**. Ignore paths off to the left - the route now continues along the Lea Navigation - continuing along the towpath with numerous sports pitches visible on Hackney Marsh to the left. Pass beneath Marshgate Bridge and a further set of road bridges, with Hackney Stadium soon visible to the left.

Shortly after passing under a railway you will reach a road bridge with a canal signpost: go left up a ramp and over the bridge. Turn left to join the Hertford Union Canal towpath. The towpath curves right and takes you past three locks and along the edge of Victoria Park. After passing under Three Colts Bridge, go right up the ramp to enter **Victoria Park** at Gunmaker's Gate. From the gate, turn left to walk along Southern Drive, with the canal still visible to your left. Leave the Park momentarily at Crown Gate East. Cross Grove Road and re-enter at Crown Gate West, walking to the left of the lake. Beyond the lake is an area called 'The Glade' and two statues of 'The Dogs of Alcibiades'. Turn left here to cross the bridge over the Regents Canal. Now, from the Bonner Gate, go half-right over Sewardstone Road and walk along Bishops Way. At the traffic lights either cross over for Cambridge Heath Railway Station or turn left and walk a further $^1/_3$ mile along Cambridge Heath Road to reach Bethnal Green Underground Station. From either station trains will return you to the start.

POINTS OF INTEREST:

Walthamstow Marsh Nature Reserve - The Reserve is one of the last surviving marshland areas in London and is now a Site of Special Scientific Interest. For hundreds of years the Marsh was Lammas Land, used for common grazing. Up to 40 species of birds breed on the Marsh and its flora includes the Adders Tongue Fern. Towards the southern end of the reserve the towpath passes under A V Roe Arches, the site of the construction of the Avro No.1 triplane by the famous aviator.

Middlesex Filter Beds Nature Reserve - This former waterworks, between the Old River Lea and the Navigation, has been imaginatively converted into wildlife habitats.

Victoria Park - A report published in 1839 stressed the need for a park in the East End and Queen Victoria encouraged its establishment. The Park which bears her name was opened in 1850 and visited by her in 1873.

REFRESHMENTS:

The Prince of Wales Inn, Lea Bridge Road.
There is a cafeteria by the lake in Victoria Park.

Walks 88 & 89　　REGENTS CANAL　　6¹⁄₂m (10¹⁄₂km)
or 9¹⁄₂m (15¹⁄₄km)

Maps: OS Sheets Landrangers 176 and 177; Pathfinder 1159.
Canal towpaths through East and Central London.
Start: At 362812, Limehouse Docklands Light Railway Station.

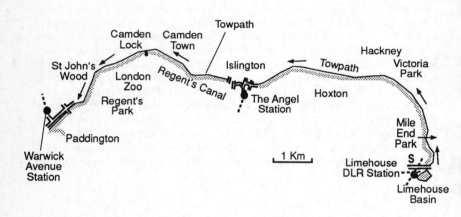

The Regents Canal provides a splendid opportunity for walkers to explore parts of London in a traffic-free environment. The towpaths feature much of social, historical, industrial and architectural interest. This route, from Limehouse to Little Venice provides examples of these various facets of the canal.

Turn right from the Limehouse DLR Station exit and right again along Commercial Road. Go under the railway bridge and, after about 300 yards, turn right down steps next to a new residential development to join the towpath. Turn right and head north towards Mile End and Hackney. The towpath passes Mile End Park and, later, follows the south-western edge of Victoria Park. It then heads through Hoxton towards Islington. On reaching Frog Lane Bridge it is necessary to divert off the towpath temporarily in order to go over the Islington Tunnel. An alternative road route is suggested on the information boards and is marked by circular iron plaques in the pavements: go over the bridge and continue on the other side of the canal. Go up the steps just before the tunnel entrance, turn briefly right, and then left into Duncan Street. Go between the York Inn and Camden Passage and turn left into Upper Street.

The shorter walk continues along Upper Street to finish at the Angel Underground Station. From there, underground trains will take you, eventually, back to the DLR and the start.

The longer walk crosses at the lights and heads down Liverpool Road. Go left down Chapel Market and, at the end, cross the pedestrian crossing and go right down Penton Street. After about 100 yards turn left down Maygood Street, then keep ahead along a paved alleyway until the canal comes into view ahead. Go through a gate on the right to regain the towpath. You soon reach St Pancra's Lock and, later, **Camden Lock.** The canal now heads towards Regent's Park: follow the towpath to the right at a small basin and walk around the northern edge of Regent's Park, with the main part of **London Zoo** visible on your left. The towpath passes through St John's Wood and, later, a short road detour is necessary: go up the stairway and along Aberdeen Place to reach the Edgware Road. Cross and walk to the right of the canal on Blomfield Road into **Little Venice.** The route ends at Westbourne Terrace Road Bridge: turn sharp right and go back along Blomfield Road. Turn left at the traffic lights to reach Warwick Avenue Underground Station from where trains return you to the start.

POINTS OF INTEREST:

Camden Lock - This area buzzes with activity and provides much of interest. Buildings of note include the 'post-modernist' GMTV premises and the Sainsbury's supermarket. The castellated lock-keeper's cottage now serves as a Regent's Canal Information Centre.

London Zoo - At one point it was feared that the zoo would have to close, but it now seems to be having something of a revival with a new emphasis on ecological and environmental issues.

Little Venice - The final stretch of canal from the Edgware Road to the Westbourne Terrace Road Bridge, where the Paddington Arm joins the Regents Canal, is particularly enjoyable. The colourfully-painted boats and the elegant canalside houses give the area a real atmosphere, even if the locality doesn't quite live up to its Venetian label!

REFRESHMENTS:

There are numerous possibilities close to the canal.

Walk 90   RUISLIP WOODS   6³/₄m (11km)

Maps: OS Sheets Landranger 176; Pathfinder 1139 and 1158.

A circular walk connecting various woodland areas.

Start: At 073890, the car park at Bayhurst Wood Country Park.

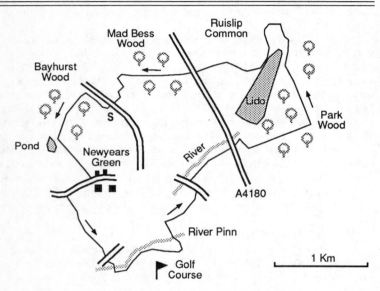

Near the car park entrance there is a bridleway marked with a blue arrow: follow this north-westwards along the edge of **Bayhurst Wood**, walking parallel to Breakspear Road North and keeping the open field to your right. Just before the path starts to go downhill, turn left along the footpath going to the centre of the woods, signed 'Hillingdon Trail'. Follow the path uphill at first, ignoring minor paths to both left and right, and then go down to the southern boundary of the wood. At this boundary, almost at the pond's edge, turn left along the smaller footpath, <u>not</u> the broader Hillingdon Trail route. Follow this path along the edge of the wood, passing a small picnic area.

    At the southern tip of the wood, turn right along a fenced bridleway to Newyears Green, ignoring stiles to the left and right. At the road, turn right and, after about 100 yards, where the road bends right, go left down a rough track. Cross a road and follow the footpath opposite. Cross the River Pinn and follow the path round to the left, passing a footbridge and going between the river and a golf course. After about 400 yards, cross another footbridge and cross the field beyond, bearing left towards a wooden hut. Cross a stile and turn right along a rather overgrown footpath beside the fence. Go past Old Clack Farm, over a stile and then bear right to rejoin the course of the river (and the Hillingdon Trail). At the next Trail sign, cross the river and take the footpath to the left, passing the rear of industrial premises and an infants school.

At the road, turn left and after about 100 yards go right down a signposted alleyway which leads into a residential road. Walk along Wallington Close to its end, where it becomes a footpath between two wooden fences. Cross a road and continue ahead across grass, keeping the stream to your right. Cross the main road, with care, go right for about 50 yards and then left down the bridleway, next to the Athletic Club, to reach the edge of Park Wood. As you enter the woods, bear half-right along a bridleway. This curves left and continues into the centre of the wood: follow the blue bridleway signs ahead for about $^1/_2$ mile and, at the second major crossing of paths, turn left. Follow this prominent track northwards until it heads downhill and you arrive at a fenced-in miniature railway. Now turn right and follow a path, keeping the railway to your left.

After passing Haste Hill Station platform, do not go right along the wide, sandy bridleway: instead, continue ahead through a gap in the wooden fence. Turn left and follow the path along the edge of **Ruislip Common.** At the fork, keep left, walking with a fence to your left. Cross a gravel bridleway and follow the permissive path into Copse Wood (the remainder of the walk coincides with the Hillingdon Trail). Follow the brown marker posts through the woods to reach a stile at Ducks Hill Road. Cross the road, with care, and go over another stile to enter the intriguingly-named 'Mad Bess Wood'. Follow the path straight through the wood, ignoring all paths to the left and right, for about $^1/_2$ mile, until a Hillingdon Trail sign directs you to the left. Now follow the wooden marker posts to the edge of the wood: the trail emerges opposite the entrance to Bayhurst Wood car park.

POINTS OF INTEREST:
Bayhurst Wood - A country park, with picnic areas and a nature trail.
Ruislip Common - The Common lies between Park Wood and Copse Wood. Poors Field supports a variety of plants including Orchid, Hare Bell and Heather.

REFRESHMENTS:
None on the route, the nearest being in Ruislip High Street.

Walk 91   GRAND UNION CANAL   6³/₄m (11km)

Maps: OS Sheets Landranger 176; Pathfinder 1174.
A walk along the Brentford Arm of the Grand Union Canal.
Start: At 174778, Brentford Railway Station.

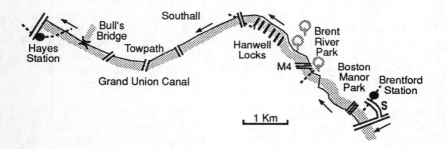

This route provides fairly easy walking along a six mile stretch of the Brentford Arm of the Grand Union Canal. It starts from Brentford Railway Station (trains run here from Waterloo) and finishes at Hayes Railway Station: this is not on the same line as Brentford, but it is relatively easy to catch a train back to central London, linking with a number of Underground lines at Paddington.

From the station exit at Brentford, cross and go left down Boston Manor Road. After about ¹/₄ mile you will reach the traffic lights at Brentford High Street: turn right and walk a further ¹/₄ mile to Brentford Bridge. Turn right at the far end of the bridge to join the Grand Union Canal towpath.

The towpath runs to the left of Brentford Gauging Lock and then passes under some overhanging buildings, under a railway line and beneath the Great West Road. Soon the greenery of Boston Manor Park can be seen on the other side of the canal.

The walker now passes a lock and a series of weirs, and then crosses the canal by means of an iron bridge called Gallows Bridge. Continue along the towpath, going under another railway bridge and the M4 road bridge. There are then various points of entry to **Brent River Park** on the right.

Walk past Osterley Lock and along a footbridge over a weir where the River Brent joins the canal. About $^2/_3$ mile further on a stone bridge marks the start of **Hanwell Locks** (veer right just before the bridge if you need refreshments – the Fox Inn is close by). Walk up the incline past the locks – the building to the right is Ealing Hospital – and then go over a railway and under a road simultaneously!

Go past another lock and walk under Glade Lane Bridge to reach Norwood Top Lock. Continue along the canal for a further $^1/_2$ mile or so to reach Wolf Bridge (with the Lamb Inn close by). From the bridge, continue along the canal towpath for a further $1^1/_2$ miles or so, passing under two more road bridges and then crossing Bull's Bridge over the Paddington Arm of the Grand Union Canal. A further $^1/_2$ mile from this point you will pass under a railway bridge: stay on the lower path to reach the road bridge at Hayes. Go up the steps and turn left. Walk along the road for about 250 yards to reach Hayes Station.

POINTS OF INTEREST:

Brent River Park – The stretch of water near here was once reputed to be the most polluted section of the canal. Now, however, the area is greatly improved and, sandwiched between the River Brent and the canal, the River Park contains woodland and riverside wildlife habitats.

Hanwell Locks – There are six locks in all, raising the canal by over 50 feet. Parts of the towpath and some of the locksides were restored in 1995.

REFRESHMENTS:

The Beehive, Brentford High Street.
The Fox, Green Lane, Hanwell.
The Lamb, Wolf's Bridge.

Walk 92   RICHMOND AND HAM   7m (11¼km)

Maps: OS Sheets Landranger 176; Pathfinder 1174.

A stroll on the Thames Path, visiting historic Ham House.

Start: At 181752, Richmond Station (Rail and Underground).

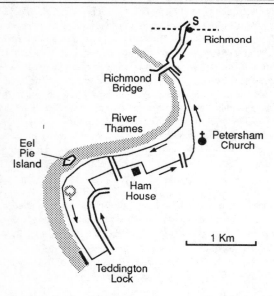

From the station, turn left along Kew Street, Richmond's main shopping thoroughfare, and follow the signs for the river. Just after the main road bears left, turn right down Water Lane for your first sight of the Thames. Here turn left, passing under Richmond Bridge, and continuing along the Thames Path. The Path is now followed for approximately three miles to Teddington Lock.

Walk through Buccleuch Gardens and rejoin the riverside path as it passes Glover Island. Look behind at this point for a view of Richmond Hill. Continue past Petersham Lodge Woods, Ham Meadows, Eel Pie Island (complete with houses and gardens) and Young Mariners Lock, to reach **Teddington Lock**.

Go past the lock and turn left at the footbridge, going along a path away from the river. On reaching a road, turn left to begin the return journey to Richmond, via Ham and Petersham, following the pavement around the edge of the meadows.

Go past a sign for 'Thames Young Mariners' and, at the end of the fence, turn left along a footpath, passing a 'Ham Lands' information board. After about 30 yards, fork right along a re⎯onably well-defined grass track. Keep on this for about 400 yards to reach a crossroads of grass tracks. Here turn right and follow the track to emerge at a large open field. Bear half-right across the field, where kestrels may be seen, to reach a lane and the entrance to **Ham House**. By now the River Thames is in view again, to your left.

Go through the entrance gate and along the drive (also a bridleway) past the splendid house and gardens. Follow the drive around to the right and then go left at the corner of the polo field, where the drive becomes a straight tarmac path. Go past the gatehouse to reach a road. Turn right, then left down Meadow Close, passing the Fox and Duck Inn. Continue down the footpath at the end of the Close, cross a road and follow the path opposite past St Peter's Church, the parish church of Petersham. Continue ahead across the meadows back to the riverside. Now retrace your steps back to Richmond Bridge and the station.

POINTS OF INTEREST:

Teddington Lock – This is actually made up of three locks, including one that is known as the 'coffin lock' because of its unusual shape. These are the lowest locks on the non-tidal section of the River Thames.

Ham House – The house, now administered by the National Trust, was built in 1610: most of what remains is 17th-century. It was lived in by the Earls of Dysart from 1637. It now contains fine tapestries, sculptures and period furniture. There is also a rare 17th-century formal garden.

REFRESHMENTS:

The Waterman's Arms, Water Lane.

Christie's Tavern, Hill Rise, Richmond Bridge.

There are many other inns, restaurants and cafes in Richmond where the walk starts and finishes.

Maps: OS Sheets Landranger 187; Pathfinder 1207 and 1208.
Demanding downland trails.
Start: At 435568, the Spinning Wheel Restaurant at Hawley's
Corner, off the A233 between Biggin Hill and Westerham.

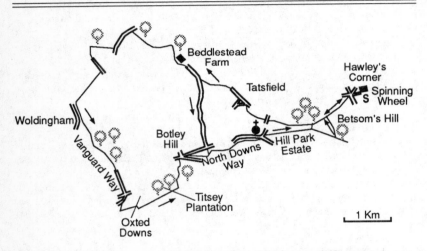

Cross the A233, with care, and head down Tatsfield Lane and Chestnut Avenue.
After nearly ½ mile this drive turns to tarmac: keep ahead for a further 200 yards,
then bear right along a signed footpath, by a stile. The path skirts the edge of a wood.
At the golf course do not go forward or right along the tracks: instead, keep ahead
and walk on the grass to the right of the line of trees. This path soon becomes a track
and where this curves left, go down a bank on to a road. Walk left for 50 yards and
then right up steps. Go over a stile on to a fenced path. When the fencing ends, keep
ahead over two stiles to reach a road. Turn left and cross the small green in front of
the Old Ship. Follow the path to the right of the pond and cross the green. At the end,
go ahead along the residential road and, when this begins to ascend, go left through a
gate on to a bridleway. Keep to the right of the next two fields, descending steeply in
the second. Go through a gate and walk diagonally across the next field to its far
corner.

The shorter route turns left here, following the lane for nearly a mile to reach the B2024. At the B2024, cross over and go ahead along a signed path. After 150 yards this meets the North Downs Way between two stiles. Turn left to rejoin the longer route.

The longer route goes right. After 300 yards, bear left, at a bridleway sign, through a gate, and cross the field corner to go through a gate. Go left, briefly, and then right along the bridleway. Level with the wood's end, go left along the bridleway, which descends and then rises. Continue to reach a road close to a transmission mast. Turn left and, after $^1/_4$ mile, go right along a bridleway which passes two more masts and continues between hegderows. At the major crossing of paths, turn left along a grass track to reach a road. Go left, then cross and go right over a stile and along a path, just beyond Worms Heath Cottages. Keep the hedge and the fence on your left and descend into a valley. Cross a farm track and keep ahead over the hill. Walk left beside a road on a permissive track (part of the Vanguard Way), then, when the road goes right, keep ahead, following the bridleway next to the track for over a mile to reach a crossroads. Go ahead, towards Oxted, forking left along a path after about 120 yards. Go over a stile on to **Oxted Downs** and down the steep hill. Turn left at a signpost to join the North Downs Way. Now follow the acorn symbols across the downs and along the edge of the Titsey Plantation. Go over a stile at the edge of a wood, down steps and then left, uphill, along a track through the woods. At the top, cross a road and go right at the sign to follow a woodland path close to the road for about $^1/_2$ mile. Now go left up steps rejoining the shorter route where there are two stiles close together.

Cross a road and go along field edges to reach a signed stile. Go left up steps, cross the B2024 and head down Chestnut Avenue. Walk past the **Hill Park Estate** and, after $^1/_2$ mile, where the road forks, keep right. A mileage stone marks the Surrey-Kent boundary. About $^1/_4$ mile further on, turn left at a stile on to a footpath over Betsom's Hill. At the end, turn right and follow the lane back to Hawley's Corner.

POINTS OF INTEREST:

Oxted Downs – This National Trust area is a good example of chalk downland. The slope also provides a superb view south.

Hill Park Estate – This includes a nature trail which illustrates the changing nature of downland habitats and landscapes.

REFRESHMENTS:

Spinning Wheel, Hawley's Corner.
The Old Ship, Ship Hill, Tatsfield.

Walk 95   CHEAM AND EWELL   7m (11¹/₄km)

Maps: OS Sheets Landranger 176; Pathfinder 1191.

Two 'villages' and Nonsuch Park.

Start: At 243638, Library Car Park, Park Road, Cheam.

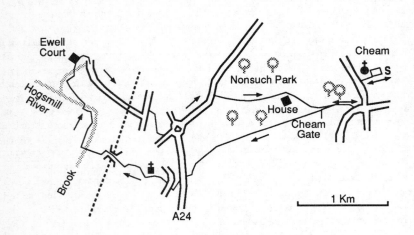

Leave the car park by the corner next to the lych-gate to reach the Broadway. Turn left and cross to visit the **Whitehall**. Continue along the Broadway to the traffic lights and turn right down Ewell Road. Cross Park Lane and enter Cheam Park beyond the public conveniences. Follow the footpath leftwards, keeping parallel with Ewell Road, to reach the Cheam Gate entrance to **Nonsuch Park**.

Now continue along the park road, passing a white barrier. Keep on this broad, tree-lined tarmac path for about ¹/₂ mile to reach a house and a junction of paths. Fork left, and then leave the tarmac, continuing ahead along a footpath between the trees. At a crossing of paths, keep forward and downhill to reach the A24. Cross, with care, and follow the pavement to the left. After about 100 yards, fork right, between a fence and a school sign, along a footpath. Follow the path for about 60 yards to reach a footpath crossing. Turn right to walk between the fence of the school fields and a number of back gardens, eventually emerging at a road opposite a disused church tower. Cross and follow the paved path past the tower and across the churchyard. Walk to the left of the church and turn left, and then right, down Kingston Road. At the village pond, cross Kingston Road and walk down Chessington Road. Shortly, where the road bends left, turn right to walk along Old School Lane. Pass Priory Court and continue ahead along the small tarmac footpath that leads to a railway bridge.

Go over the bridge to reach a road. Turn left, then, between houses 57 and 61, take a tarmac path with green verges, on the right. Follow this path, crossing two roads to reach a brook. Turn right and walk beside the brook, crossing it at the second bridge. Now keep to the grass by the brook, curving left where it joins the Hogsmill River. Cross the river by means of the five round steps and turn left immediately along the footpath running along its northern bank. Shortly, next to a wooden footbridge, turn right along a tarmac footpath. Where there is a gate in the wire fence on the left, use it to enter the grounds of Ewell Court. Follow the path around the edge of the lake and, at the lake's far end, cross a footbridge, go through the gate and turn left to rejoin the footpath you followed previously.

After about 50 yards, at a T-junction of paths, turn right. Go straight over Manor Drive and walk ahead, along Meadow Walk, for about $^1/_3$ mile. Where the road bends left, continue forward under the railway bridge and along an unmade road. At the main road, turn left to head up Beggars Hill. Just after the Jolly Waggoners Inn, cross over and turn right into Shortcroft Road. Now follow the footpath across the recreation field to reach a road. Turn left to reach the Organ Crossroads. Cross the Ewell by-pass, carefully, and continue along London Road for $^1/_3$ mile to reach the entrance gate to Nonsuch Park on the right. Go through the gate at the left hand corner of the car park and head diagonally across the large field beyond to its far corner. From the gate there, continue along a grass track, walking to the right of a plantation and then keeping forward to reach the Mansion House. Follow the path past the front of the house, then keep right to go behind the building. From 'Fir Walk', head diagonally across a field to reach Cheam Gate and from there retrace your steps back to Cheam Park, the Broadway and the Library Car Park.

POINTS OF INTEREST:
Whitehall – This white, weatherboarded house dates from the 16th century.
Nonsuch Park – Henry VIII's Nonsuch Palace no longer exists, but there is a 19th-century Mansion House and 300 acres of parkland.

REFRESHMENTS:
Ye Olde Red Lion, a 15th-century Inn in Park Road, Cheam.

Walk 96   **WALTHAM ABBEY** $7\frac{1}{2}$m (12km)

Maps: OS Sheets Landranger 177; Pathfinder 1140 and 1120.
A walk along navigation towpaths and through a Country Park.
Start: At 372982, the River Lee, Swan and Pike Pool Car Park
close to Enfield Lock.

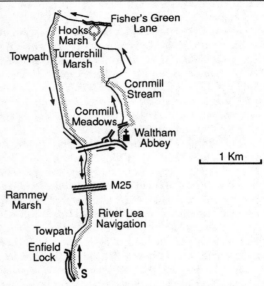

Start from the car park a short distance north of **Enfield Lock** (about $\frac{1}{2}$ mile from
Enfield Lock railway station). The walk follows the River Lea towpath to Waltham
Abbey, completes a circuit of the marshes north of Waltham Abbey and returns on
the Navigation towpath.

From the car park, walk to the riverside and turn right at the signpost indicating
'Waltham Abbey 3.0 km'. Go over a bridge, cross a road and walk to the other side of
the Navigation at Enfield Lock. From here the towpath runs along the western side of
the River Lea all the way to Waltham Abbey.

The towpath takes you past the Greyhound Inn and under a footbridge, with
Rammey Marsh on your left. After about a further $\frac{1}{2}$ mile the path reaches Rammey

Marsh Lock and then passes under the M25 motorway. Continue for a further $\frac{1}{2}$ mile to reach the Hazlemere Marina and the Old English Gentleman Inn. Leave the towpath here, going up the ramp and turning right on to the road bridge. Continue along the road towards **Waltham Abbey**. Just before the Abbey tower, cross and go left where there is a public footpath sign. Go over a small wooden bridge and then turn right to cross a red-brick bridge. Now walk under the Gatehouse Archways (the Lea Valley Countryside Park Information Centre is ahead) and turn left along the path by the river, passing a number of mosaic creatures in the grass. Cross the river by means of a wooden bridge and use a subway to go under the road. Turn right, and then go left, just before the bridge, through a wooden kissing gate into Cornmill Meadows Dragonfly Sanctuary. Follow the path by Cornmill Stream for nearly $\frac{1}{2}$ mile until a bridge appears on the right. Cross this, turn left and follow the path beside a wire fence.

The path detours away from the stream in order to go around a government research establishment: follow the high wire fence to the left and then left again. When you reach the corner of a field, keep ahead to cross a small wooden bridge and continue along the path to Fishers Green Lane, as indicated by the marker post. Soon you reach the end of the wire fence: bear half-left along the footpath to Hooks Marsh. This goes across a field, approaches the stream and then turns right to reach Fishers Green Lane. Turn left and, shortly, cross two bridges to reach a large car park at Hooks Marsh. Walk to the right of the wooden Hooks Marsh sign, go through a wooden gate and along a tarmac path signposted to Cheshunt. Go over a bridge and continue along the path, ignoring a left turn to Hall Marsh. Shortly you will reach a stone bridge across the Lee Navigation: cross and turn left along the towpath to head back towards Waltham Abbey. It is about $1\frac{1}{2}$ miles back to the Waltham Abbey road bridge on the towpath, passing Waltham Common and Waltham Town Locks. Continue ahead under the road bridge for a further mile to return to Enfield Lock.

POINTS OF INTEREST:

Enfield Lock – It is possible to walk south on the River Lea (or Lee) Navigation as far as the Regent's Canal in Hackney, or north into Hertfordshire. This section of the river forms the eastern boundary of Enfield. Rammey Marsh provides wildlife interest.
Waltham Abbey – The remains of the 11th-century monastery can be seen in the Abbey Gardens. King Harold's body was buried here after the Battle of Hastings.

REFRESHMENTS:

The inns mentioned in the route description can be used, and there are also possibilities in Waltham Abbey.

Walk 97   **UXBRIDGE WATERWAYS**   7¹/₂m (12km)

Maps: OS Sheets Landranger 176; Pathfinder 1158.

An interesting canal and riverside walk.

Start: At 055842, Uxbridge Underground Station.

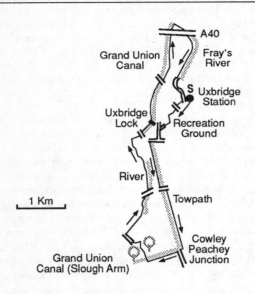

This walk forms a kind of figure of eight with alternate sections of canal and river.

From the Station, go right along the High Street and then left down Windsor Street. At the end go over Cross Street and keep ahead, passing to the right of an old churchyard. Cross two more sets of lights, then go left down Cowley Road. After about 30 yards, turn right along Wellington Road. Go over the footbridge into Rockingham Recreation Ground and then take the left-hand path beside the river. At the corner, follow the tarmac path, to the right, away from the river, going along the southern edge of the field. At the next corner, cross Frays Waye and continue down Austin Waye, turning left at the end. At the end of the road, opposite the Lord Bill Inn, turn right. Immediately after crossing a bridge, turn left down steps on to the towpath of the Grand Union Canal. At bridge No. 188, cross the road and rejoin the canal on the left-hand side, passing Cowley Lock. Pass under bridges Nos. 189 and 190 and, at **Cowley Peachey Junction**, cross the footbridge.

Follow the towpath along the Slough Arm of the canal, which includes an aqueduct, to reach another footbridge. Go up the steps to cross the bridge and continue along the bridleway to reach another footbridge next to Little Britain Lake. Cross and follow the path left, then right into a lane. Continue on this for about 350 yards, turning right over a stile on to a footpath signposted 'Colne Valley Way', just as the M25 comes into view. Follow the surfaced path, ignoring a footpath signposted to the left. Shortly, the path crosses a stream and veers left alongside the River Colne: continue along this pleasant path, passing a weir and, after a further $^1/_2$ mile, reaching a road bridge. Cross the road and the bridge, and continue along the other side of the river. The path stays by the river, with an industrial estate to the right, for about $^2/_3$ mile, then curves right to head back towards Uxbridge. Continue along an unmade road to Cowley Mill Road and turn left. Cross St Johns Road at the roundabout, and walk ahead on to the grass. Turn right and follow the riverside path behind a number of back gardens. Pass several willow trees, cross Riverside Way (opposite the General Eliott Inn) and then follow the road for a short distance, turning left just before the bridge on to the Grand Union Canal towpath.

Walk past the narrowboats and go under the Oxford Road Bridge. Use bridge No. 184 to cross and continue along the towpath on the other side of the canal from **Uxbridge Lock**. After nearly $^1/_2$ mile, you will pass under the A40 to reach a stone footbridge. Leave the canal here, turning right along the footpath. This passes under the A40 again and reaches a footbridge over a stream. Cross and stay on the path as it turns right, passes under a disused railway and follows the course of Fray's River. The path passes numerous back gardens and then joins the pavement of a residential close. At its end, turn left into High Street. Keep ahead along this to reach a pedestrianised area and Uxbridge Station.

POINTS OF INTEREST:

Cowley Peachey Junction – This is the junction of the main Grand Union canal with the Slough Arm. The main waterway continues south and east to Hayes and Brentford while it is 5 miles to Slough on the western arm.

Uxbridge Lock – The waterways are an important part of the town's history and assisted the development of Uxbridge as a market centre. The lock is a good place to watch modern day canal activities.

REFRESHMENTS:

The General Eliott, St Johns Road.

Walk 98   SUNBURY LOCK   7½m (12km)

Maps: OS Sheets Landranger 176; Pathfinder 1190.

A walk on the Surrey bank of the River Thames.

Start: At 151689, Car Park at Hampton Court Green
     or at 154683, Hampton Court Rail Station.

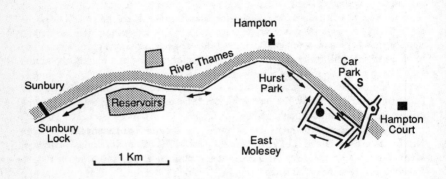

The Surrey bank of the Thames westwards from Hampton Court Bridge provides the setting for a quiet, pleasant riverside stroll with views across the river to Hampton and Sunbury.

From the car park at Hampton Court Green, walk along the Green close to Hampton Court Road. Cross at the pedestrian crossing and walk over Hampton Court Bridge, with a view of Hampton Court itself to the left. (From the station start, cross over to the northern end of Hampton Court Bridge).

From the northern end of the bridge, go right for about 30 yards and then left along Bridge Road which contains a mixture of small shops and inns. Towards the end of Bridge Road, curve right along Wolsey Road. At the end (Church Road) turn

186

right to reach St Paul's, the Parish Church of East Molesey. Walk around the church and keep ahead along Church Road to its junction with the A3050. Cross, with care, and keep ahead along Graburn Way to reach the Barge Walk and the riverside. Turn left and walk along the Thames Path through **Hurst Park.** Stay on the towpath for over two miles to reach Sunbury Lock.

There are reservoirs to the left, stylish houses across the river to the right and chalets on Sunbury Court Island. As you pass a reservoir wall with the words 'Metropolitan Water Board' inscribed on it, **Sunbury Lock** can be seen ahead. The lock is the turn-round point. It is not possible to cross the river here and the next bridge is at Walton-on-Thames, some two miles away, so unless you want a very long walk turn round and walk back towards Hampton Court.

There is usually plenty of activity on the river, especially at weekends, and the towpath provides a good walking surface. Soon you reach Hurst Park again: keep on the towpath which in the final section passes Molesey Boat Club, Hampton Court Crescent and Molesey Lock before reaching Hampton Court Bridge.

POINTS OF INTEREST:
Hurst Park – The Park is a good point from which to view the various riverside activities. There is a swan feeding area, though swans are by no means the only birds that may be seen. Garrick's Temple, Hampton Sailing Club, the Bell Inn and Hampton Church, with its prominent tower, can be seen across the river. A ferry operates between Hurst Park and Hampton.
Sunbury Lock – The main lock can be very busy and is a good place to watch boats passing through on weekend afternoons. The lock has motorised gates and in 1990 a salmon ladder was opened at Sunbury Weir.

REFRESHMENTS:
The Cardinal Wolsey, Hampton Court Road.
The Streets of London (Pub and Pizza Restaurant), Riverbank, Hampton Court.

Walk 99   **MILL HILL** $7^3/_4$m ($12^1/_2$km)

Maps: OS Sheets Landranger 176; Pathfinder 1140.

A brookside trail, parks and a disused railway.

Start: At 253907, Finchley Central Underground Station.

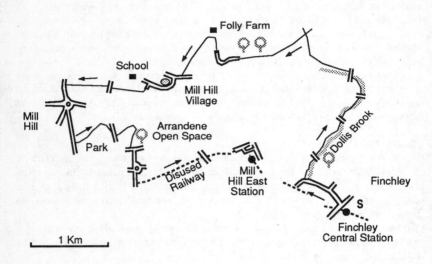

The route ends at Mill Hill East station from where there is a fairly frequent service back to Finchley.

    Leave Finchley Central Station by the Ballards Lane exit. Cross the main road at the lights and walk down Nether Street. Continue along Dollis Road, then, shortly after crossing Gordon Road, with the Mill Hill Viaduct to the left, turn right along the **Dollis Valley Greenwalk**. Follow this waymarked trail, on a tarmac path close to the brook, for over a mile. At the third road, cross, but do not go on to the grass section ahead: instead, turn right and walk along the road for 100 yards before turning left along the drive for Woodside Park Club. Keep ahead on the grass and then on a path between the brook and a bowling green. Follow this path for about $^1/_2$ mile to reach a stile in a wooden barrier. Go left, over this, and follow the path beyond uphill. Once over the hill the path reaches a gate and a stile in the corner of a field: go over the stile and bear right up a drive to reach a road. Go ahead for 150 yards, then turn right along another road, opposite Hillview Road. At the far end of the cricket field, before Folly Farm, turn left along a track. Cross a small footbridge and go diagonally left across the next field, aiming for a gap between wooden posts, just to the left of a tree in the middle of the hedge. Maintain direction diagonally across the next field. Go through the trees and over a stile halfway down the right-hand side of the field. Continue along the fenced grass footpath beyond and, at the end, go left over a stile and along a path by a stream. Go over the next stile and up the school driveway beyond. Cross a road and turn right, then bear left at Milespit Hill, passing the Mill Hill Village sign and a pond. Go right up High Street for 150 yards, and then left along Wills Grove. After 100 yards, turn right along a tarmac public footpath across **Mill Hill School** grounds to reach a road. Cross and continue along Milton Road. At the end, keep forward along another tarmac path. Turn left at the road and, as this approaches a main road, go forward along the paved path across a section of green.

Use the lights to cross the dual carriageway and follow the pavement leftwards, along the Broadway, for a short distance. Cross at the pedestrian crossing, then go half-left down Flower Lane. Follow this for about $1/_3$ mile to reach a footpath across a park on the left. The path passes under the road and continues across another section of Mill Hill Park. After passing a bowling green, turn right along a smaller tarmac path. Leave the park at the corner and turn right to walk along the road. After 20 yards, cross and turn left through a metal gate. Follow the grass path beyond up Featherstone Hill. At the top, fork right along another grass track. After 100 yards or so, just after passing between two trees, turn right along a path indicated by a marker post. The path takes you down to a road: go left, and then right down Page Street. Keep ahead at the roundabout and, after about 300 yards, bear left along a sloping footpath indicated as part of a circular walk. Go left again along the disused railway track, following it for over a mile, passing under a road bridge. After the second bridge, keep left on the grass area and walk forward along the road. Turn right at Bittacy Road and right again at the end to reach Mill Hill East Station.

POINTS OF INTEREST:
Dollis Valley Greenwalk – This 14 mile trail follows the course of the Dollis Brook in the Borough of Barnet.
Mill Hill School – The School was founded in 1807 by a group of Protestant Dissenters.

REFRESHMENTS:
There are numerous possibilities in Finchley and Mill Hill.

Walk 100   **WEALD PARK**   10m (16km)

Maps: OS Sheets Landranger 177; Pathfinder 1141.

A walk through parkland and along paths and country lanes.

Start: At 551928, the car park at Dagnam Park, Settle Road, Harold Hill.

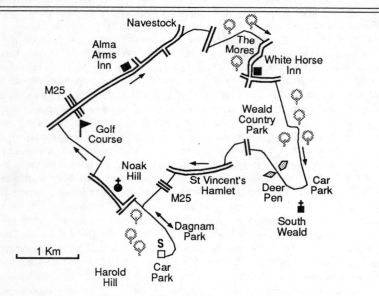

Walk back along the car park access road and, after the small building, turn left along a track across **Dagnam Park**. This track runs along the field edge and into a wooded area. When it joins a tarmac lane, continue ahead to reach Chequers Road. Cross, turn left and, after 150 yards, go right along Church Road. Walk through Noak Hill village and then turn right along Benskins Lane. After about 400 yards a signposted path to Horseman Side appears on the left: cross the stile and walk along the edge of the golf course. Continue along a gravel track to pass a four-way footpath signpost, still keeping to the edge of the golf course. Pass a green and a pond, and then cross a footbridge. The path now keeps close to the hedgerow and then continues between the 10th and 18th tees to reach a car park. Turn right and walk along the road over the M25. Continue along this road for nearly 1$^1/_2$ miles, passing the Alma Arms after about a mile. After passing the King William IV, where the road bends left, go over the stile ahead, by two footpath signs. Walk along the left-hand side of the field beyond, go over a stile and walk beside another hedgerow to reach Wheelers Lane.

Turn right and walk along the lane for about 350 yards, then go left through a gate and along a path through woodlands called 'The Mores'. Fork left initially, and then follow the main path through the woods, ignoring the paths going left to reach a road junction opposite a cottage. Turn right and walk along Mores Lane for $1/_4$ mile to reach another junction and the White Horse.

Turn left and walk along Coxtie Green Road. After about 500 yards, just after Gate House, turn right along a gravel lane into **Weald Country Park**. Where a bridleway crosses, keep ahead to pass between two woods. When the track reaches a T-junction with another major track, turn left and, after nearly 200 yards, turn right down an avenue of chestnut trees. At the end, go forward through a gate and cross a stream. Keep ahead along the grass path going uphill, forking right where this divides. The path takes you over a hill and a stile into the Bluebell Pond Picnic Area: go through the gate into the car parking area and immediately turn right. Walk between the wooden posts and up the hill, going up the steps to reach the top.

Go down the other side of the hill, passing to the right of a car park. At the bottom, keep ahead on the grass, with a wall visible to the left. Shortly, pass to the right of another car park to join a tree-lined gravel path that heads downhill past a deer pen and between two lakes. After crossing the small bridge, maintain direction along the grass path up the hill signposted 'Toilets'. Go to the left of a pond and then turn left along a gravel drive. At the North Avenue exit of Weald Park, turn right along a road and, after 150 yards, left along a tarmac drive. When this reaches another road, go right to walk through St Vincent's Hamlet. After just over $1/_2$ mile, before Old MacDonald's Farm Park, turn left along Wrightsbridge Road. This passes under the M25 and soon joins the footpath back to Dagnam Park.

POINTS OF INTEREST:
Dagnam Park – A small country park including a fishing lake and Hatter's Wood.
Weald Country Park – A popular recreational area, the Park contains two lakes, several woods and open fields, a deer pen and a horse/cycle circuit.

REFRESHMENTS:
The Alma Arms, Navestock.
The White Horse, Coxtie Green.

TITLES IN THE SERIES